Facilitation in Action

Finding Your Authentic Training Style

ATD's Facilitator Team

Carrie Addington, Jared Douglas,
Nikki O'Keeffe, and Darryl Wyles

PRESS

Alexandria, VA

ATD Press is an internationally renowned source of insightful and practical
information on talent development, training, and professional development.

ATD Press
1640 King Street
Alexandria, VA 22314 USA

Ordering information: Books published by ATD Press can be purchased by visiting ATD's website at td.org/books or by calling 800.628.2783 or 703.683.8100.

Library of Congress Control Number: 2022939951

ISBN-10: 1-953946-36-4
ISBN-13: 978-1-953946-36-2
e-ISBN: 978-1-953946-37-9

ATD Press Editorial Staff
Director: Sarah Halgas
Manager: Melissa Jones
Content Manager: Eliza Blanchard
Developmental Editor: Jack Harlow
Production Editor: Hannah Sternberg
Text Design: Shirley E.M. Raybuck
Cover Design: Rose Richey

Printed by BR Printers, San Jose, CA

For all the learners we've encountered in our careers,
you have taught us just as much as we've taught you.

For all our fellow trainers who have shaped our own journeys.

Contents

Authors' Note

Writing *Facilitation in Action* was a collaborative labor of love among four master ATD facilitators, who came together to write a book that guides facilitators in continually honing and developing their skills in an ever-evolving capability.

Collectively, we have 55 years of facilitation experience across 22 ATD Education programs and have reached more than 7,000 ATD learners across various segments, including government, healthcare, technology, media, transportation, and retail. We facilitate ATD's train-the-trainer programs, where we hear so often how insular and autonomous the role of a trainer or facilitator can be. What our participants end up valuing most about these programs is the opportunity to come together with colleagues and share ideas and experiences, to build a sense of camaraderie, and to learn from one another's unique experiences through shared stories and examples. While the four of us are aligned in our approach to facilitation, we also make room for the unique style and approach that each of us favors. In short, there's no one way to facilitate, and that's what this book hopes to explore with you.

So, with that value in mind, with that hunger for more stories and examples to help turn concepts into practical application, we immediately thought of how our various perspectives, facilitation styles, and approaches to key topics in our field would provide a rich cache of stories and techniques for consideration in your own work.

Whom Is This Book For?

As new facilitators, we began our careers by watching other trainers and facilitators in action; by gathering all the checklists, tips, and common practices we could find; and by diligently studying. We absorbed intently in the hopes of embodying what other people's definitions of *good* and *impactful* looked like. We checked off all the checklists we could find as we began developing skills. While this continues to be a worthwhile approach, especially at the start of a training career, the moments we learned the most from were the stories and practical examples shared by other trainers—the ideas we gathered from being creative and practical with those who do what we do every day.

This book aims to be a trainer's how-to, a trainer's manifesto, a trainer's call to arms, a trainer's celebration and assessment of where we've come from and where we're going. It's for new and aspiring trainers who are looking to learn from other trainers. It's also a book for those who are established in the field and looking for new and different approaches to trusted methodologies and attitudes. It's for any learning and development professional who wants to hear stories, examples, and practical tips that open your thinking around the impact a facilitator and trainer can have.

You may notice we toggle between *facilitator* and *trainer* at times. There are nuances that differentiate the two roles, but for the purposes of this book we will use them interchangeably. Whether you identify as a trainer or a facilitator, or both, depending on the programs you're delivering, we are speaking to you when we use the word *facilitator*.

Our Approach to Facilitation

When we are facilitating, we are in constant communication with our learners. We are working alongside them in their exploration, hearing what they have to say and implementing their needs into the experience. We are coaching and guiding them to find their own path to walk during and after the experience. Our mindset is crucial to preparation because facilitation is organic, collaborative, and sometimes messy.

If we asked you to name a great facilitator, you would most likely identify someone you had an impactful experience with (our own lists are very long). That is because facilitation is personal. In facilitation, we want to break down tangible and intangible barriers between us and our learners.

This book will guide you through the process of deepening your thinking and developing your skills in training and facilitation. There are a plethora of "best practices" that infiltrate the industry. To be clear, we have nothing against best practices. The term was first introduced as a spin-off from the original "best method or procedure" in the early 1980s. And, the industry has been using this terminology for almost half a century to mean "a procedure that has been shown by research and experience to produce optimal results and that is established or proposed as a standard suitable for widespread adoption" (*Merriam-Webster*). No wonder we continue to find them, use them, and respond to them. There are, in fact, best practices in our field, and in a role that is largely dependent on the people it serves, it's our call to challenge best practices, evolve the field, and create new approaches based on what we learn from those we work with. We aim to explore common or proven practices that can be used to clarify your approach, not define it.

What to Expect in This Book

Writing *Facilitation in Action* was an opportunity to redefine how we think of honing our training delivery and facilitation skills in the dynamic landscape that is learning and development. We'll provide our considerations and stories, which are rooted in practical experience and application, not only from our tenure as facilitators at ATD but from our own backgrounds spanning industries from government and healthcare to marketing and beauty.

We present a lot of questions and offer our varying perspectives for your consideration, and we provide tools and templates that start as lists but invite you to take what we've shared and apply it in your own work.

Each chapter is structured around subtopics, posed as questions. These questions are actual learner questions that we've received over our years as facilitators conducting train-the-trainer programs. Questions that, in the moment of hearing them, raised deeper and broader questions for us as facilitators as well. The participants who attend our programs challenge our thinking regularly with their viewpoints, their insightful questions, and their desire to acquire a deeper level of expertise in their role; this structure was a way to honor the learners we've had the great pleasure of working alongside over the years. You can read the book in the order we've laid it out or skip around based on your preferred topic; the journey is yours.

Chapter 1 kicks off with developing a facilitation mindset, one that embraces a growth mindset and focuses on what your learners can achieve and what they need to be successful.

Chapter 2 is all about setting the stage for learners ahead of time, from environment setup to communications, and preparing yourself to ensure the learning experience is engaging and outcome-oriented.

Chapter 3 delves into the role of the facilitator, from being a department of one and creating positive environments for learning, to scaling your delivery for different group sizes and understanding your role in workplace performance.

Chapter 4 focuses on developing your unique facilitation style and building confidence in your approach.

Chapter 5 explores adapting your facilitation across various modalities (virtual, face-to-face, asynchronous, blended).

Chapter 6 looks at how to have the greatest impact through a learner-centric approach, while remaining flexible enough to pivot and adapt in the moment to learner needs.

Chapter 7 discusses the importance of empathy and inclusion to facilitation, with tips for modifying your verbal and nonverbal communication as well as some activities.

Chapter 8 dives into the art of feedback: how to deliver it and how to receive it.

Chapter 9 ties the discussion of the facilitator's role and impact together with an inspection of how to ensure learners' performance improvement.

Chapter 10 wraps up with a look to the future of facilitation and how we as facilitators can stay future-focused and remain lifelong learners.

Throughout the book there are moments of interaction for you, the reader, to engage with, either as a reflection tool after your next training delivery, at your next train-the-trainer book club, or even at your local ATD chapter event or team meeting. Fold the pages, highlight meaningful passages, write in the margins—do whatever you need to engage with the content. At the end of each chapter, we'll leave you with an invitation to reflect on considerations and questions that will help you define and intentionally live in your role as a trainer and facilitator. Because at the end of the day, nothing prepares a trainer better for the role of training delivery than another trainer.

With continued admiration on your learning journey,
Carrie, Jared, Nikki, and Darryl

Meet Your Facilitators

"How did you get started?" This question is a consistent one that we hear in our training programs. We all want to know the origin story, the path each person took to get to where they are today. How we began directly affects where we go, so it's important to consider how you got started in the profession. It's also worth exploring how there's no one right way to become an impactful facilitator.

We'll start.

How did you get started in training and development?

Carrie Addington: Very carefully.

I was working for Esteé Lauder Companies in a field sales position, where I partnered with small-business owners to provide education and business consulting. I found myself gravitating to the education part of the role more so than the sales or business consulting.

The haircare brand I worked for had a university housed within the corporate offices in the heart of the Meatpacking District in NYC, where business owners, managers, and staff would come from around the globe to learn about business strategy and professional development. Day one on the job, I stated to a co-worker that I would be teaching at the university before it was all said and done. It wasn't premeditated, and I hadn't had that plan when I'd accepted the role; I just naturally felt called to that as I oriented myself within the company. I watched the transformational experience of that learning space, the tangible representation of partnership between a brand and its customers, and I became more and more drawn to facilitation. I volunteered to teach at the university in addition to my sales position and took that time to be a sponge and soak up everything I could from that experience.

The career sweet spot (that moment when I realized, like a small spark ignited within, this is what I'm meant to do) happened at our annual sales gathering, when I co-facilitated a program in front of 100 peers and the company executives. During those two hours, something came alive in me, and I felt more connected to the people in the room through the learning experience. That's the magic, I suppose. Training and developing others is a whole category of human connection separate from any other method, and I was hooked.

Jared Douglas: Very intentionally.

I was in graduate school studying industrial organizational psychology, and I did an internship with the Metropolitan Transportation Authority (MTA) in NYC in their training and development department. I learned so much and absorbed a variety of training programs, from new hire orientations with 100 people in attendance to manager development programs. During this internship, observing the vast scope of training and how it set people up for success, I realized my love of communication, people, and leader development, and that's when I decided to pursue this field that I'd fallen in love with. One day, my manager missed the Long Island train, and I stepped into the new manager program as the facilitator. I was thrown into the deep end of the pool and had to swim.

I also received some great advice early on. I started in training and development as a designer and had a mentor who said, "Anyone can be a 'good' facilitator or designer. If you want to be great at either, you must become fluent in both."

Nikki O'Keeffe: With sheer determination, really.

I had always wanted to be a teacher, but for some reason delayed stepping into that role initially, telling myself, "I'll do that later," as if

I knew it would be waiting for me. I was living in Australia counseling international students when I found myself building a growing curiosity for how to support the students outside our one-on-one conversations. Everyone needs to learn how to make friends when they don't speak the language, so I started creating opportunities for learning and mentoring based on a gap and a need.

Years later, I moved back to the United States and was working in software project management and building systems for drug trials, and the technical focus of it was not filling me up like the curiosity and connection that I had established in my work in Australia. I wanted to help others. I wanted to mentor people. As good timing would have it, I saw an opening for a trainer and was definitive in my thought: "This is my job; this is what I have to do."

The funny part of the story is that I went into labor with my first child during my first interview for the role. I told myself and my husband, "I'm not going into labor; I'm going into that interview." I spent my first week with my first child creating a slide deck around the importance of a needs assessment to continue the interview process. I knew I wanted the job, and I was determined to get it. (I did, by the way.)

Darryl Wyles: I'm an accidental trainer.

I initially struggled at my job as a banker and my manager said I needed assistance to improve performance. They paired me with someone to get me up to speed quickly, and my performance improved dramatically from this approach. Soon, I was succeeding at the job, and all I could focus on was helping others who were facing similar challenges. Before long, I got the opportunity to participate in a project as a trainer (thanks to a company merger). The training department at the financial institution noticed my efforts and asked me to apply for a role in their department. I fell in love with training and participating in the growth of others. Ever since, I've been focused on learning and helping others grow.

What topic do you love to facilitate?

Carrie: Facilitation and train-the-trainer programs, daring facilitation, overcoming challenging classroom behaviors, and leadership development programs.

Jared: Communication skills and instructional design principles (both the science and the art).

Nikki: Train-the-trainer programs and instructional design.

Darryl: Management development.

How has facilitation changed you?

Carrie: It's made me a better human and is my way of connecting with others. It's crafted and personalized my leadership style.

Jared: Facilitation has given me confidence as a subject matter expert (SME)—building expertise, exuding expertise, and managing to convince learners immediately that you are an expert. To do so, you must convince yourself first.

Nikki: Hearing expert advice from learners I work with. We, as facilitators, don't know it all.

Darryl: Facilitation has broadened my world perspective thanks to the people I meet. I love creating an environment where people come together and forge bonds.

What's your point of difference (POD) as a facilitator?

Carrie: My focus on the uniqueness of each individual in the room and my love of language and the arts contribute to work with individuals on establishing deeper connections with their daily work.

Jared: Establishing safety and comfort for learning to happen. I care about the learners a lot.

Nikki: Thoughtful and caring—at the root, the learners are humans who value connection first.

Darryl: I think training programs are great mini networking opportunities.

How would you define your facilitation style?

Carrie: Structured, service-minded, practical, and impactful.

Jared: Learner-centric, purpose-driven (I hate busy work), and casual.

Nikki: Energetic.

Darryl: A smooth, cool vibe.

What's the perspective you'll be bringing to the topics covered in this book?

Carrie: Challenging our thinking on key facilitation topics. I ask myself often, "What's different that I haven't heard before that's going to help me challenge and elevate our thinking?" I focus on the importance of mindset shifting, coaching, and questioning. Imagine empathy married with practicality.

Jared: I'm going to fight Carrie for some things because we are so similar in so many ways, but how we do facilitation is different. I'm focused on practical approaches—are we providing tips readers can use tomorrow for micro-adjustments and quick wins?

Nikki: I want to motivate readers to incorporate previous skills sets and lean on confidence from prior experience. Encourage readers to try new techniques and have fun. Model respect and your learners will follow.

Darryl: Your skill set can work across multiple industries. It's all about creating a productive learning environment.

● ● ●

These are our stories—well, at least the beginning of them. Throughout the rest of the book, you'll read more practical examples of our experiences on all things facilitation. And as you can tell, while we share similarities, our perspectives are our own and deeply unique.

Now it's your turn! Over the course of this book, we want you to reflect on your facilitation style; how we begin directly affects where we go, so it's important to consider how you got started in the profession. What is your origin story?

Chapter 1
The Facilitation Mindset

Being intentional with our mindset is at the core of our role as trainers and facilitators. It matters not only *what* we think, but *how* we think as we guide learners through a learning experience. So, it's only fitting that we open a book on training and facilitation with a conversation about mindset.

Ryan Gottfredson (2022) delved into research to make the argument that the effectiveness of a talent development professional "hinges upon your mindset," or how we view the world. For facilitators and trainers, our world most often includes the learning experience, the learners, and the content. So, in short, our mindset affects everything we do.

When the four of us facilitate ATD's train-the-trainer programs, and as we reflect on our early careers as trainers, there is a constant focus on "getting it right." This includes following all the checklists and best practices that tell us how to successfully meet the objectives of the program and demonstrate skill in training delivery. We want to deliver the content, adapt to our learners, overcome challenges, and even remove those pesky filler words we've grown accustomed to using when our nerves get the best of us. We want to provide our learners with the information they need and engage them with impactful questions and discussions. We want what they learn to translate into workplace performance improvements that impact the business. These are important skills to manage and master, but these alone can leave us feeling like merely a conduit for information and, over time, our function can start to feel—dare we say—mechanical.

At one point it may have been enough to be a conduit for information, and in certain contexts it may still be, but for most trainers and facilitators our role demands we go a step further. Questions like "What does this mean for you?" or "How does this impact your daily work?" are some of the most powerful in our toolkit. We take the objective content we are exploring and support learners as they contextualize and connect individual meaning to what they are learning. So, what does our mindset have to do with that?

Well, a lot. What is possible if we don't focus so much on "getting it right"? What happens when our foundational facilitation skills become developed, sharpened, and easier to use? This is when we elevate from good to great and when our mindset expands, adding dimension and depth to our facilitation.

A Tale of Two Mindsets

We can't have a conversation about mindset without referencing Carol Dweck (2007). As a psychologist and researcher for 30 years on the topic of developmental psychology, Dweck demystifies the two mindsets we confront as humans: a fixed mindset and a growth mindset (Table 1-1).

Table 1-1. Fixed vs. Growth Mindset

Mindset	What It Is	How It Presents
Fixed Mindset	Belief that your qualities are set in stone.	Creates an urgency to prove yourself over and over.
Growth Mindset	Belief that your qualities are things you can cultivate through your efforts, your strategies, and help from others.	The basic qualities you possess are a starting point for development.

Adapted from Dweck (2007).

You might wonder, how does this apply to facilitation? What does a fixed or growth mindset look like in our facilitator minds?

Well, it looks like this: Early in her training career, after executing a failed jigsaw activity, Carrie convinced herself (á la a fixed mindset) that she couldn't conquer this sometimes challenging activity. Her inner dialogue anytime a jigsaw was used as an instructional method in a course was "I'm not smart enough to get this right," "I'm not good with numbers," and "I'm going to damage my credibility if I mess this up." She had to work overtime to move from a fixed mindset to a growth mindset. Now, she conducts jigsaw activities, and while they're not easy for her, if something goes awry, she responds with "I should consider using a visual analogy to help explain the activity (for the learners and for me)," or "I have more opportunities to get this right," or even "My challenge with this technique is relatable to the learners and builds trust."

The challenging thing about mindset is that we can very easily backslide into a fixed mindset as facilitators in moments when negative self-talk creeps in, almost without us recognizing. However, we can learn to uphold a growth mindset even while having individual thoughts that are more fixed. When it comes to your role as a trainer or facilitator, what type of mindset do you have? If we place mindset on a continuum, where would you place yourself? To pose the question in a different way, what belief do you have in yourself? Write your initials on the continuum in Figure 1-1 (not where you want to be but where you are).

Figure 1-1. Mindset Continuum

Fixed Mindset ➤ Growth Mindset

Now that we know where we are starting, let's explore how we move from good to great. (Hint: Regardless of where you placed yourself on the continuum above, there's always opportunity for growth.)

How Do I Move From Good to Great?

The Ritz Carlton prides itself on customer service in the luxury hotel space (NIST 2015). The brand has been celebrated and revered in the customer service industry for defining the gold standard of service. It empowers its employees to live the company's values by establishing a strong foundation of guiding principles, including a company motto, three essential service steps, a credo statement, and an employee promise. To uphold this level of service-oriented greatness, the Credo Card is designed to be a part of the employees' uniform as a reinforcement of their foundational standards. This is supplemented with brief, daily touch-base meetings to discuss how to uphold their service. We, as facilitators, are also always thinking of how to elevate from good to great. The Ritz Carlton's service-oriented approach is an inspiration for how to do just that.

This type of work takes more self-management than we may initially realize. Adopting a service-minded perspective can help us to focus on our learners' needs for sure, but we can't completely overlook our own needs along the way. We need a second focus on developing our own skills to ensure we continue to grow and develop.

The concept of growth in our roles is challenging because there's no real endgame for facilitators. There's no peak to reach where you are greeted with magical beaches, refreshing drinks with tiny umbrellas, and the ability to rest in your acquired skills; instead, the industry is always evolving, the people in the room (virtual or in-person) are continually changing, and our considerations and environments are constantly shifting. We must remain curious about what is new, what is next, and even what isn't working anymore if we want to continue to create impactful learning experiences.

After all, the role of a facilitator is to create opportunities for learning, opportunities that our learners want to seize. We prepare content and experiences, but a large part of our success is dependent on our relationship with learners and how we hold them *able*.

For Your Consideration

Moving From Good to Great

Consider these tips for elevating your facilitation.

- ▶ **Take on or volunteer to train a new topic to stretch your skill set.** Early in Darryl's career in retail banking, he trained bank tellers and built his confidence in this space. To grow his skill set, he volunteered to facilitate training for the company's wealth management units, stretching him to learn about new systems, new clients, and a segment of the workforce he wasn't familiar with. Volunteering for this opportunity helped sharpen the skills he uses to prepare for new training initiatives.

- **Observe other facilitators in action.** This enables you to view a learning session from two points of view: the facilitator and the learner. Whether you watch a colleague or attend a session at a conference, these are opportunities to see common facilitation skills modeled and to identify nuances of a particular facilitation style along the way. Also, it gives you an opportunity to view how learners receive and respond to information shared.
- **Read books and articles on facilitation skills and techniques.** The road to where we want to go often has already been traveled by someone else. Reading books and articles from thought leaders exposes you to new perspectives that can inform your planning and decision making in the classroom. Read and study broadly and aim to continually connect with other facilitators.
- **Periodically, take a facilitation skills self-assessment.** We constantly evolve. Completing a self-assessment gives you a snapshot of where you are today and highlights the opportunities for growth you have moving forward. Build a schedule where you set time aside to do a self-assessment as part of your preparation process for training delivery.
- **Take risks.** Don't be afraid to challenge yourself and get away from your comfort zone. After spending 15 years in retail banking, Darryl transitioned to working for a parks and recreation agency. The change in workforce and workflow was different from what he was accustomed to in retail banking, and allowed him to adjust his facilitation approach to fit within the agency's culture. Instead of delivering classes in hotels or conference rooms, he delivered classes at a maintenance facility or a nature center. While the setting changed, the expectations his learners had for him remained the same.

How Do I Hold Learners Able as Opposed to Accountable?

Part of the facilitation mindset is the language we use to connect individuals to information. The words we use have innate and sometimes unexpected power (which we explore more in chapter 7). Sometimes our mindset influences our language, and sometimes our language influences our mindset. *Accountable* is an example of the latter.

Consider your reaction to the word *accountable*. Do you tense at all? Perhaps you roll your eyes, or even get flushed or feel frustrated. Whatever happens for you, it's an example of how language influences your mindset and the power of words in triggering emotions and reactions. The same happens for learners when we are facilitating. Our goal is to open their minds to possibilities, so our language is crucial to making sure we don't unintentionally shut them down, render them passive, or distract them.

Shifting from *accountable* to *able* with our learners is a subtle yet important example of this concept. *Ableness* has a positive connotation because it is rooted in what our learners can do as opposed to what we think they should do. Table 1-2 gives a few examples of a simple shift from *accountable* to *able*.

Table 1-2. Accountable vs. Able

Accountable	Able
Did you complete the activity?	Did you have everything you needed to complete the activity?
Did you use the feedback model in the role play?	What was challenging about using the feedback model for the first time?
You will need to score 80% to pass this assessment.	A passing score is 80% on this assessment. What additional support do you need to be successful?

It is a subtle but important shift that is rooted in mindset. Holding learners able includes using language oriented toward opportunity and how they are set up for success. We are giving learners the opportunity to share not just if they did something, but how they did it, and perhaps even what could have improved the experience too. Accountability is a transactional approach (tasks and deadlines), whereas ableness is a collaborative approach (ideas and parameters).

Ableness focuses on what's possible, what our learners can achieve and what they need to be successful. This is a powerful focus for us as facilitators because we can guide our learners down this path with us. We can ask them questions to encourage thinking in this pattern of ableness during the learning experience, which could have a lasting impact when they are back on the job. If we adopt a mindset of ableness, it could influence our learners to approach their own work with a mindset of ableness. We can even apply the concept of ableness over accountability when we encounter one of the biggest challenges in facilitation: pivoting mid-course.

How Do I Get Better at Pivoting in the Moment When Facilitating?

When we talk about pivoting during facilitation, we are referencing those unexpected moments that occur that require you as the facilitator to adapt to keep the learning experience on track. In fact, you'll find that as we explore various topics throughout this book, a common theme is modeling adaptability and perfecting the pivot in your facilitation. This ranks high on our "frequent questions from learners" list, regardless of what program we are facilitating.

Pivoting is equal parts intuition and planning because, at its very core, facilitation is adaptation. Yes, we plan content, and we also plan to be ready to throw it all out if it isn't working for our learners. Sometimes, at the proverbial fork in the road, neither path works, and we need to turn right around and march back up the road we just walked.

When we prepare to adapt, what role does mindset play? What are we thinking about and how are we anticipating and approaching the work that we do? These are abstract questions that we invite you to revisit. They are not easily answered, but they are crucial for facilitators to consider for every program we deliver, marking the ability to pivot or adapt as an essential skill for facilitators.

When we are facilitating, we are in constant conversation with our learners. We are working alongside them in their exploration, hearing what they have to say and incorporating their needs into the experience. We are coaching and guiding them to find their own path to walk during and after the experience. Facilitation is organic, sometimes messy, sometimes collaborative, so our mindset is particularly important in preparing us to adapt. To prepare ourselves for the pivot, we typically think through the following questions:

- What feelings do I have around pivoting?
- What's at risk if I pivot? If I don't pivot?
- What's the ideal outcome?
- What behaviors or specific facilitation skills can I leverage in this moment?

Facilitation in Action

Feedback as an Enabler for Mindset

Early in her facilitation journey, Carrie was leading a 60-minute course for small-business owners and managers on managing profit and loss statements. Her audience was captive, and her organization was the leading authority on business trainings in the beauty industry for its particular segment. A mentor observed from the back of the room as Carrie facilitated the content, exactly as the facilitator materials dictated. The content was delivered on time and as expected. The learners were gracious as they departed the room for the next session and remarked on how much they enjoyed Carrie's facilitation style.

As the last participant departed the room, Carrie was beaming and feeling confident in her performance. Her mentor asked if she was open to feedback. The mentor pointed out that while the delivery was on time, accurate, and informational, the experience and practicality of the content was lacking. Her mentor pointed out that Carrie had added no relevant examples or personal stories to illuminate the content and that when a few questions were posed by the learners, she'd answered with a promise to follow up instead of taking those questions in the moment. Carrie nodded and was ready to defend her choice when her mentor asked her a simple question: "You know to include stories and questions for increased engagement and retention, so why did you make the decision you did?" Carrie sat quietly before uttering, "I was scared it would mess up my plan." The pivot didn't happen, not because of a lack of skill or knowledge but a lack of willingness (mindset) and preparedness. It's this moment that shifted Carrie's mindset to constantly invite formative feedback from learners and peers and plan for how to overcome in the moment. Today, nearly 15 years later, Carrie embraces those moments, thriving when a kink is thrown into the plan, challenging her to adjust in the moment. The mantra she uses to keep herself on track is "It's not about me! It's about the learner."

What Is the Difference Between Training and Facilitation, Really?

If context and preparation are crucial to our mindset, we need to understand what different contexts we may be called to prepare for. As we stated in the introduction, it is quite possible to identify as both a trainer and a facilitator depending on the training program, the content, the organization, and the intended outcomes. Recognizing the difference between training and facilitation and when to leverage each is an art. Let's take an opportunity to define each (*Merriam-Webster*).

Facilitate (verb): To make easier, help bring about.

Train (verb): To make prepared (as by exercise) for a test of skill.

For a more learning-specific definition of *facilitation*, we can turn to the Talent Development Body of Knowledge (2019):

Facilitator: takes less of a delivery role, is learner-centered, and acts as a catalyst for learning

Trainer: a TD professional who helps individuals improve performance by facilitating learning in a traditional or virtual classroom, one-on-one, or on-the-job in an organization

The definitions help to illuminate a rather clear distinction between the two. **Facilitation** is about getting learners comfortable in the environment so they can discover their own takeaways. We might have learning objectives and ideas of what learners will walk away with after a facilitation, but we also remain open to being surprised with new or alternative ideas or perspectives. Consider this, and reread this paragraph. Identify the words and phrases that resonate with you.

Training is a very collaborative form of information delivery. When we train, we usually teach specific processes and procedures and ensure that our learners comprehend the information and can replicate the skill or process we are covering. Training tends to work with higher-risk scenarios like software training, safety regulations, and new hire training. These areas have content that is specific in nature, containing fact and fallacy, and right and wrong ways to do things. Not following the proper safety measures when operating heavy machinery in a manufacturing environment has very dangerous and specific consequences: People will be injured and equipment will be damaged or destroyed. Now, consider rereading this paragraph and highlighting all the words that resonate with you. How many words and phrases resonate with your daily work?

It's likely that you identify with one more than the other by the very nature of the type of training programs you deliver. When conducting field training for a premier beauty brand, Carrie was a trainer because her role was to share the right information, to inform, and to drive performance through information delivery. When conducting learning programs focused on developing leadership narratives, Carrie was a facilitator because her role was to listen, question, and coach as well as build consensus.

The content, the learners, and the experience of our learning programs all might require us to toggle between these two roles often.

Consolidating the differences and situational nuances of the trainer's role and the facilitator's role is filled with "what if's." ATD provides an overview of some of the core differences in the snapshot in Table 1-3.

Table 1-3. Training vs. Facilitating Roles

The Trainer's Role	The Facilitator's Role
Shares the right information	Shares content in a learner-centered way
Offers clear point of view	Serves as a catalyst for learning
Champions content	Champions experience
Instructs, directs, and informs	Listens, questions, and coaches to allow learners to derive meaning
Ensures learning takes place	Builds consensus
Drives learning objective achievement	Drives action and relevance to enhance learning

Adapted from ATD (2016).

We, the authors of this book, identify most as facilitators and will use that language throughout the book to encapsulate both facilitators and trainers, regardless of which role you more closely identify with.

For Your Consideration

We Don't Know What We Don't Know

Imagine you are facilitating a leadership workshop where learners took a 360 assessment of their leadership abilities, submitted their self-assessment, and collected feedback from their peers, teams, and leaders. Each learner receives a different report highlighting their unique strengths and weaknesses. That means each learner has something different to focus on, yet they are all attending the same workshop with you.

How will you make this work? How do you run one workshop with a myriad of outcomes for your learners? This is one of the key differences between training and facilitating. When we facilitate, we do not always know how we'll guide the learners to the outcomes. We provide the content and the opportunity for them to devise significant meaning for themselves, while serving as a guide or coach.

In this example, we would most likely introduce learners to the leadership model we are working with, help them digest their reports to understand their results, then support their exploration to identify key opportunities to strengthen their leadership abilities. We move past the specific takeaway from us or the course and into a contextualized plan that is learner generated.

Having a general understanding of the difference between training and facilitating is important because we all gravitate toward our own preferences. One of the most impactful learning moments in our experience facilitating ATD's Training & Facilitation Certificate Program is a lesson that uses Elaine Biech's Four Dimensions of Training to identify the dimensions we as facilitators focus on when delivering programs (Biech 2005). Those four dimensions are:

- **Content:** The purpose or goal of the learning experience
- **Process:** The overall flow of a training program
- **Task:** The tasks needed to manage the learning environment
- **People:** The participants in the training program

There are a variety of approaches to take in facilitating this content, but regardless of the facilitator's approach, this is one of the highest rated and remarked-on activities. It gets such a high response because it's actionable and a great mechanism for not only evaluating your facilitation approach but planning for ways to continue your own professional development.

Think about your style when you are working with learners. Do you tend to focus on the mechanics of a workshop, putting time and effort into the setup of activities? Perhaps you always have one eye on the clock to make sure you cover everything in your agenda. Maybe you hear yourself saying, "I'm going to pause here to make sure we are all clear on this point before moving on." If any of these scenarios sound familiar, you are probably focused on the tasks and processes involved in a workshop; this may indicate a preference for the dimensions of task and process.

Do you find yourself getting very excited about your subject matter? Maybe losing track of time as you move from topic to topic? Do you hear yourself asking questions that yield responses with more feelings or opinions rather than facts? If you answered yes to any of those questions, you are probably focused on the content and people when facilitating and may have a preference for the dimensions of content and people.

Natural preferences are just that: *natural*. It doesn't matter which category we lean toward if we are aware of where our preferences push us, so we can pull from the other dimensions whenever it benefits our learners. The art is moving between the four dimensions of training to weave an experience for our learners that feels seamless and provides a more balanced approach. For instance, the experience in the next Facilitation in Action section encompasses many of the ideas we have discussed in this chapter.

Facilitation in Action

A Day in the Life

"I have an update for you," Jane, the stakeholder, said to Jared.

"Oh?" Jared replied, his head cocked to the side. It was 8:30 a.m. and he had just arrived in the Chicago office ready to facilitate a team-building workshop for Jane's team of 15.

"We got approval to fly the extended team in for today!" Jane said. She was beaming, excited by this development.

"Well, that's great news! How many people are we expecting now?" Jared asked nervously as they rounded the corner to the main conference room, which was buzzing with people.

"We're close to 40 now," Jane said, her smile shrinking a little as she turned to him. "Is that going to work for what you had planned?" she asked.

"We'll figure it out," he said with a smile.

Jared was in a bit of a dilemma. Jane's team had recently partnered with a new creative team and there was a little friction between them. They didn't know each other, worked in different cities and offices, and didn't even use the same terms and concepts because their day-to-day work was quite different.

The original training plan was to travel to Chicago to conduct on-site training for Jane's team in communication and relationship-building tactics to make headway with their creative counterparts. The workshop Jared had planned would have equipped learners with tools to develop relationships. Now, with both teams in the same room, the purpose had changed. Jared could go beyond equipping individuals with tools—he could develop actual relationships in the moment of the learning experience.

Jared's mind was already racing, and his mindset needed to shift quickly. He began thinking of what he had prepared and what he could still use. What activities or content could he keep? What could he change to be more effective? How could he manage the logistics of almost triple the number of learners he had been expecting?

Jared used the preparation time he had left to adapt the beginning of his plan. As a facilitator, he was very purpose focused. That meant he needed to be crystal-clear on why everyone was together, and he wanted to ensure that his learners could walk away feeling like they could immediately apply what they had learned or do at least one thing differently or better than before.

Most of the content was relevant because they were still there to learn how to work better with one another. The format changed drastically, though. Many learners were meeting their counterparts face-to-face for the first time. Jared gave more time to introductions, knowing it was an investment in their relationships and would build rapport.

Because there was some existing tension between the teams, he knew the learners needed to spend a good amount of time exploring communication styles and preferences. He leaned heavily into his training skills when exploring the styles, ensuring they understood the model, and switched into facilitation when trying to pull preferences from everyone. He adapted as many activities as possible to partner each learner with someone new they were working with. They shifted from learning about developing relationships to building them together in the moment.

He printed extra materials and took the workshop one section at a time. While learners worked through an activity, he used that time to adapt what would come next. It was challenging, a true test of flexibility and creativity, but it became one of the most powerful and memorable experiences he's had as a facilitator. And he attributed his success to his facilitation mindset.

Jared thought of how to hold the learners able on two measures: Were they practicing adapting their communication styles? And, were they getting to know their colleagues better? He chose these two measures because they were possible to accomplish in the room and they were possible to observe as a facilitator. Throughout the workshop he used debriefs to ask questions and hear from learners what their experiences had been. This helped inform along the way how their relationships were dweveloping and what they needed in the next activity or discussion.

The day was a success both in formal and informal measurements. Many learners shared in their evaluations that they'd learned a new skill and felt a new appreciation for different styles and perspectives when communicating. On the informal side, his stakeholders were happy and felt the day was energizing and productive. Most of the team members went out to happy hour together after the training, which, after spending a full eight hours together, says something about the relationships they were already building. They literally didn't want to stop communicating when the workday was done.

In this example, Jared's mindset focused on the practical. He made choices that yielded immediate results for his learners; they developed relationships with their new colleagues that very day. This story is not unique; every day, facilitators face changes in circumstances or last-minute requests. While we may handle similar situations in different ways, we are all capable of being successful.

What's Next?

Being intentional with our mindset means taking a physical and mental breath, thinking about where we are in the moment and where we want to be in the next moment, and making decisions that get us closer to the desired outcome. This admittedly can be difficult. It requires fierce control over our emotions, reactions, biases, and impulses, yet also a dash of spontaneity and trust in ourselves.

Our mindset is not stagnant; it is something ever-changing that adapts to our context. We can, however, practice shifting our mindset. We can find a comfortable or productive place for our mind to rest, and we can practice getting it there with different techniques. One technique is to explore more about ourselves and our preferences.

In the Authors' Note to this book, each of us answered a series of questions to demonstrate our preferences and experiences, and how we view our individual styles as facilitators. You can use the same questions to begin exploring your facilitation mindset. Where are you starting from? What are your natural preferences? Being aware of yourself will influence your relationship with your content, your learners, and the learning experience you create.

Invitation

Answer these questions to explore your mindset and preferences. Feel free to review the authors' responses in the Authors' Note to prompt your thinking.

1. What topics do I love to facilitate ?

   _____

   _____

2. How has facilitation changed me?

   _____

   _____

3. What is my point of difference as a facilitator?

   _____

   _____

4. What are three words that define my unique facilitation style?

_____

_____

Chapter 2
Setting the Stage for Learning

Taking the time and giving attention to "setting the stage" before a training delivery is the single most effective thing you can do as a facilitator to influence the tone of your learning experiences. Setting the stage includes all the expectation setting and rallying around a course experience that you do before coming together in a formal learning environment.

What Do I Need to Do to Set the Stage?

At ATD, we subscribe to the belief that facilitation is equal parts preparation and delivery. Let's review a few key categories to consider when setting the stage and preparing for training delivery.

Environment

The environment includes any consideration of the physical space (face-to-face or live online) where learning is taking place. For the **face-to-face classroom**, this includes setting the temperature, rearranging waste receptacles, and positioning wall charts. It also includes the table arrangement and layout, the space between seats, the flow of traffic between tables and around the room, and the presentation of the facilitator table. To help create the ideal face-to-face environment, Carrie walks the space several times. First, she walks it to familiarize herself with the functionality of the space, testing outlets, temperature controls, and lighting switches. Then she walks it with a lens of the learner, thinking, "What will they see first, second, third when they arrive for the training?" She moves waste bins to a less obvious location, she ensures the Wi-Fi code is displayed at the front of the room, she lays out supplies for herself and learners, and she familiarizes herself with emergency procedures, restrooms, and nearby eateries. The key is anticipating the learners' needs and ensuring the space is prepared with them in mind.

For the **live online classroom**, managing the environment means coordinating with your producer (if you have that extra support) prior to the course to discuss how you will work together in the classroom; testing the technology, including the audio and video components; and practicing screenshare and any additional features you'll need to use in your live online platform. Nikki maintains that equally important in the live online classroom is setting up your facilitation space. We have a general rule on our team that your "setup" at your desk translates directly to what learners hear and see in the virtual classroom. This includes having a timing chart displayed in eyesight of your webcam to reference throughout the program and ensure you are tracking with the timing. Additional components of our workspace include a water bottle nearby, facilitator notes, the participant roster, the participant workbook, and typically a guiding focus scribbled on a sticky note in front of us that reads "Have fun" or "Slow down" or "Make a difference."

Technology

Test videos and audio files using the system in your classroom . . . several times. For the face-to-face classroom, test power outlets, projector USB cables, wireless clickers, microphones, or any additional technological equipment, like virtual reality headsets or applications that let learners experience augmented reality. As a team, we aim to test two to three times, and even then we anticipate there will be snags. Take time to plan for the "what if" scenarios when it comes to tech. In the live online classroom, test your Wi-Fi connection, webcam, audio and headset, and all platform features that you will leverage during your training.

Tone

What do you want your learners to think the moment they step in the room? Do you want to be feverishly writing wall charts when they arrive? Do you want to be unpacking materials? Or do you want the room set and organized, allowing them to enter with confidence instead of questions? Music, lighting, and messaging all make a difference. And as we say on our team, "A cluttered room invites a cluttered mind."

Lighting and Audio

We generally aim to set lighting and audio lower and adjust them higher once learners are in the room and we've surveyed their comfort. Imagine sitting in a classroom and the first audio that plays over the loudspeaker blasts across the room, making you jump from your chair. Or the lights are so bright that you immediately flash back to your school days and begin feeling the onset of a headache. Start at a lower setting and ensure that your learners are comfortable with the level of sound and light. It's good to keep in mind that lighting and audio can also compromise the comfort of learners who suffer from migraines or seizures.

Personal Comfort

The best thing you can do to prepare for learners' personal comfort is mention it in pre-course communications emails. As a best practice, our team includes a note regarding temperature in our pre-course communications email to let learners know that we'll aim to make everyone as comfortable as possible, but if you know you are sensitive to climate controls, we encourage bringing a light jacket or sweater. See the sample communication to learners later in this chapter for the specific language we use.

Materials

Display your materials, with an emphasis on *display*. Distribute materials (as applicable) before learners enter the room as opposed to passing them out during instruction. This allows them to begin the experience knowing what we are giving them to be successful. Ensure you have your materials out as well, including facilitator guide, timing charts, participant roster, and any activity supplies. For learning experiences that leverage digital materials, make sure to communicate any bring-your-own-device (BYOD) requirements ahead of time and plan for the possibility that someone may arrive without the technology they need. For live online learning, have your files easily attainable if you need to resend anything to learners in the midst of instruction or an activity.

Host, Producer, and Learner Communication

Reach out early and often. For the **face-to-face classroom,** you might have a program host or sponsor (or you might be that person too). We make it a practice to email one or two weeks prior to the program to connect and clarify any logistical questions and align on what time we can get into the space to set up for the training.

For the **live online classroom,** you might have a virtual producer who is your technical support on the back end of the program. At ATD, we have a team of learning delivery specialists who are the magical superheroes of our virtual classroom. To ensure we work collaboratively and effectively throughout the session, we have an email communication template that is used to align with the producer prior to delivery to discuss preferences in facilitation style, moments of assistance needed from the producer, how we will communicate privately during the session, and preferences on engagement. This goes a long way for not only aligning on our approach to facilitating the course but preparing ourselves for each session. And because we are asked often for these tools, we've included sample templated language for these communications in this chapter to get you started.

For all programs, you have learners. We may rely on the logistical teams in our training department, technology platforms, or automated processes that alert learners to the information they need to know before, during, and after a training. However, as facilitators, we can take specific action to set expectations, gain learner buy-in, and promote intrigue toward the training. We can send logistical details, questions, and materials or blogs that spark interest, and begin making connections to the content for the learners through informal conversations.

Self

Last but not least, you must prepare *yourself* as much as you prepare all the elements already described. As facilitators we function in a constant pivot; we are doing one thing and thinking of six others most of the time. What will you do to ensure you prepare yourself for the delivery as well? What do you need to be successful? Carrie does prior planning to ensure she is ready to facilitate 30 minutes before the first participant could arrive. This allows her time to set her intentions for the program and visualize a successful outcome. Darryl ensures he is prepared in advance to allow time to connect one-on-one with each participant as they arrive, because those relationships are core to his style. Whether it's a power pose, a preparation ritual, or a text to your team right before you start to announce excitement and feel camaraderie (we're guilty!), ensure you are preparing yourself.

And part of how you prepare yourself is communicating with those you'll interact with in the course. Let's look at some templates for communicating with the facilities host, producer, and learners. Customizing these templates for your own programs will ensure consistency across trainers (if you are lucky enough to work alongside a team of trainers), and it will positively affect the learner experience.

Sample Setup Communication: Virtual Producer

Lillian: Good afternoon! I hope this finds you doing well. I'm so excited to finally get to work with you next week for [Course Name], [Date, Hours, Time Zone].

We have a current total of 22 participants across six roles. We will have one auditor of the program who will observing only and will not participate in breakout sessions.

The materials I'll be using are located here and version [Enter version]:
[Include link or attached file]

Day One Logistics:
(Add any logistical considerations that are live online platform specific as needed.)
- I'll be there and logged in with my coffee right at 9:30 a.m.
- I have posted a communication to learners to remind them of pre-work and provide my contact information.
- Slide 34, with the instructions for sharing your screen, passing host controls, always seems to be a snag for learners. Would you be able to help ensure that goes smoothly by detailing instructions prior to the activity?
- Two learners have emailed prior to the course stating they'll be coming from another training and will arrive right on time or shortly after our start time. Will you help me welcome them behind the scenes in chat?

Day One Activities:
- Exercise 1.2: [Exercise Name] breakout groups should be sorted 3–4 in a group. Producer will load a copy of Proposal B in the breakout rooms for participants to work with. Please save their work and bring back to main room for debrief.
- Exercise 1.3: [Exercise Name] Independent activity, no producer action needed.
- Exercise 1.4: [Exercise Name] Breakout groups 3–4 in a group. Producer will load a blank whiteboard in each breakout room. Please save their work and bring back to main room for debrief.
- Exercise 2.3: [Exercise Name]: Part 1: Independent activity, no producer action needed. Part 2: Pairs in breakouts to share work and provide feedback. In the case of an odd number, I'll be paired with someone in a breakout, and you will need to bounce to other breakouts to ensure everyone is on track.
- Exercise 3.1: [Exercise Name]: Breakout groups, two groups total. Producer will load a blank whiteboard in each breakout room. Save their work and bring back to main room for debrief.

Facilitator Preferences:

Since this is our first time working together, I wanted to share some insights and gather thoughts from you on how we can best work together in support of the learners.

- To communicate during the session, I prefer we message outside of the platform to avoid any miscommunications in the course itself. Please confirm this approach and let me know your suggested communication tool.
- I'm almost ALWAYS behind time, so no need for time checks from you as I have a printed-off timing sheet and am constantly monitoring on my end! Where I do ask for your help in timing is on activities—I'll adjust timing as needed for exercises, and I'll need you to let me and the learners know when time is up, please. I lose track of time quickly in exercises because I'm engaging with the content and learners. You can message me privately with 5 minutes remaining in an activity and you can give participants 1 minute verbal warnings on timing for activities.
- I need the most assistance with reminding participants in chat where they can find the materials we are using for exercises.

Let me know if you have any additional thoughts, and I look forward to hearing your thoughts on how we can partner in this program.

[Name]

[Email]

[Phone]

Sample Setup Communication: Host (Face-to-Face Program)

(Note: This is a sample message to a host at a facility. You may tailor depending on if you are using an external facility or internal resource.)

Seema: Good afternoon! My name is [Name], and I'm the facilitator who will be on-site next week [Dates] from [Time] for [Program].

I wanted to reach out ahead of time and introduce myself. Additionally, I wanted to ask a few clarifying questions so I can ensure I'm prepared:

- Can you please confirm receipt of the materials that were set to arrive on Tuesday of this week for the program?
- Can you confirm a convenient time for you when I can enter the room for setup, either the morning of the program or the evening prior? I can be flexible with your schedule.
- I wanted to confirm that the tables of the room will be set up in pods with four seats at each pod.
- Can you confirm that you will have a technology support contact on-site during the program? Is it possible to receive his name and how best to alert him when assistance is needed?
- Most importantly, how do you start your morning? Coffee, tea, green juice?

Thank you in advance and I look forward to meeting you! My full contact information is listed below.

[Name]

[Phone]

[Email]

Sample Setup Communication: Learner (Face-to-Face Program)

Good mid-morning! My name is [Name], and I have the pleasure of being your facilitator for [Program Name] starting on [Day, Date, Times, Time Zone] each day in [Location] located at [Address].

One of my favorite things about this program is [Enter Detail] because it has helped me [Enter Benefit of Course Topic].

- Now would be a great time to log on to the LMS and confirm you are ready for our time together. Please be sure you have fully prepared for the course. This requires you to:
- Post on Welcome & Introductions. Tell us who you are, where you work, what your role is, what you aim to learn from our three days together, and one fun detail about yourself.
- Review the documents posted under the Pre-Work tab.
- Select a real-life project to bring to our sessions. As we work through the course, you will have a chance to reference a project you're working on.

We will be supplying some morning and afternoon snacks, but if you have particular dietary needs, we suggest packing a light snack. You will have an hour for lunch each day and there are a few nearby quick spots for eats that we can suggest upon arrival. We aim to keep everyone comfortable in the classroom with our temperature settings, but if you run cold (as I do), please bring an extra layer.

Public parking is available in the parking garage attached to the building, or you can use street parking as available.

Please feel free to reach out with any questions, as I aim to be a continued resource for you. I look forward to meeting you and working with you.
[Name]
[Email]
[Phone]

What If My Learners Don't Use the Pre-Work to Prepare?

Pre-work is an informal activity or assignment learners are encouraged or required to complete before a formal learning event. Pre-work could be assigning articles or texts to read before a session, a self-assessment, a call for identification of a work project to bring to the training, or even a piece of the content that sets the baseline of knowledge before entering the course experience.

Regardless of the form it takes, there are two primary functions of pre-work for learners:

- To familiarize or introduce learners to content
- To engage learners in the learning experience

Pre-work leverages adult learning principles by establishing relevance for the learner and tapping into self-motivation. It also gives us the opportunity to expand the learning experience beyond the classroom (virtual or in-person). It can turn the learning switch on in learners' brains to generate interest and curiosity in the content.

So, what happens if learners do not complete assigned pre-work? Here are a few potential options to accommodate them and retain the value of the learning experience:

- Use the introduction or beginning of class to explore the content or pre-work.
- Provide a high-level overview. Ask learners who completed the pre-work to share their thoughts and contributions.
- If the pre-work was intended to inform individual activities, turn some of the content and activities into conversations or group work for collaboration.
- Extend breaks or lunch periods for individual exploration or guided demonstrations.

For Your Consideration

No time for pre-work? No problem.

Before running a feedback workshop for managers at a marketing firm, Jared sends pre-work in the form of prompts. One question reads: "Think of a time you received feedback that was very impactful, and a time you received feedback that felt counterproductive. What was different between those two experiences?"

Asking questions that leverage learners' experiences primes their brains to consider their relationship with the content, which can create richer conversations throughout the workshop and enhance learning transfer back to their roles.

Is pre-work a prerequisite for attending the course? If yes, how strict can or should we be when enforcing the rule? For example, imagine you are facilitating a workshop on communication and behavioral preferences. The pre-work is taking a self-assessment that yields a report. The report will be shared during the workshop so learners can explore the communication and behavioral concepts in general while also understanding their unique preferences. In this case, pre-work is mandatory to fully contribute to the learning experience.

This is—and should be—a rare occurrence. As facilitators, our role is to provide opportunities to learn. By adding in too many or very complex prerequisites, we inhibit our ability to provide those opportunities and inadvertently create barriers for some learners.

The majority of ATD Education programs are designed with pre-work being conditional, and as facilitators we prepare with that in mind. We are ready to weave the pre-work into our facilitation of the content and also prepared for the likelihood that an individual or the group was unable to complete it. There is no single right place or time to use pre-work, but it is a powerful tool in any facilitator's toolbox if leveraged appropriately. Here are a few practical tips to using pre-work in your learning experiences.

Determine a Distribution Method

Often facilitators choose to send an introduction email to learners ahead of time. This could be an excellent opportunity to share any pre-work they need to complete. If learners are using technology or a learning platform during the experience, pre-work could serve as an introduction to the environment they will be working in.

Define Clear Expectations

What does "good" look like within the parameters of the pre-work? Do learners need to submit anything ahead of time? Do they need to share anything with the facilitator or fellow learners? Is it required or optional? What prerequisites exist, if any? Provide as much clarity as possible regarding the requirements so learners can be successful in their preparation for learning.

Allow Time Proportional to the Assignment

Reading an article is a much simpler task than completing a 360-degree feedback assessment. Factor in the level of effort from learners (and others) when developing your timeline for pre-work. More effort means more time needed to complete the exercise.

Use Pre-Work as an Engagement Technique

Fundamentally, pre-work exists to support content, but it can also enhance engagement. Use the opportunity to generate excitement around the topic or experience. Pulling on learners' experiences in pre-work assignments can create a sense of relevance and interest in the content.

How Do You Prepare to Facilitate? What's Your Process?

Preparing learners for learning is important, and so is preparing ourselves. The more prepared we are for the learning experience, the better it will be for our learners. Earlier we mentioned pre-work has two primary functions for learners: to familiarize or introduce learners to content and to engage learners in the learning experience.

It also has a very beneficial function for facilitators. Reviewing any assignments or contributions generated by learners during pre-work can provide us insight into learners' current knowledge and skill level. While this can get us geared up for the content, there are a few key categories to consider as we prepare for any given learning experience: content, logistics, and self.

Know Your Content

Think of a speaker or facilitator you witnessed that displayed a deep understanding of their content. Their body language was probably relaxed but intentional, their voice clear and energetic. This is because there is a relationship between our content knowledge and confidence when we facilitate.

It is common to be nervous before facilitating, but we can remove many of the destructive thoughts and self-doubts with proper preparation. Preparation is your best response to the inner critic. When we are very familiar with our content, we can begin to self-edit thoughts or concerns that we don't know what we're doing. We can begin to replace them with positive thoughts, thinking: "I know my plan; I am prepared for this."

Here are a few tips to prepare your content:

- **Read.** Review the facilitator and participant guide in its entirety. That's right, start to finish, top to bottom, introduction to conclusion. It will do wonders for preparing your flow, pace, and transitions. When time is against you in this effort (as it often is), begin with the course outcomes, then review the modules and lessons that build the program. Once you're familiar, then you can dive deeper into the specifics. If we expect our learners to move through the content, we must be able to as well. While reading your content, ask yourself, "How can I bring this to life in an authentic way?"

- **Practice. Practice. Practice.** Then do it again. And again. While practice technically impacts every facet of preparation, it is critical for learning your content. The more familiar you are with your content, the less you will need facilitator guides, notes, or reference materials, and the more this will boost your confidence. Record your practice—with both video and audio—to identify different growth opportunities (you'll spot different things from a video than you will from an audio recording). Apps like Speeko or Ummo provide broader awareness and high-level feedback of your presentation style, tracking your pace, filler words, pausing, intonation, articulations, and even word choice.

- **Plan examples and stories.** If you are facilitating a topic, chances are you have practical experiences that can be shared through storytelling. What opportunities exist in the content to provide an example or a story? What concepts or ideas would benefit from an illustration? Plan and rehearse relevant stories to be ready to offer them to learners during the experience. Many times, your stories will uncover related anecdotes from your learners. If you're short on your own stories, reach out to a colleague to share theirs: "My colleague experienced. . . ."

- **Anticipate needs.** As your learners move through the content with you, what questions will they have? What barriers might exist for them to comprehend or apply the subject matter?

Consider as many options as possible to illuminate challenges before they become an actual problem in the learning experience. What can you do to mitigate them ahead of time or in the moment?

- **Reflect and review.** If you have presented this content before, ask yourself what you want to do better this time. What questions were you unable to answer in the moment? What details did you miss? If you haven't presented this content before, is there anyone you can reach out to who has? Who is available to help you prepare? When Darryl first began facilitating a coaching program in support of an organizational initiative to foster innovative programming among employees, the content and the course design was new to him. After facilitating more than 30 instances of that program, he adopted an almost habitual reflect and review process where he'd identify learner responses to various sections of the content. Because of this effort, he was able to better anticipate the moments where learners are most challenged. He became versed not only in what was being taught in the program, but how he needed to teach it because the reach to hundreds of learners had demonstrated the potential gaps in learning.

Prepare Logistics

If content is what your learners will be doing, logistics are how your learners will be doing it. Expert facilitators move between discussions, activities, and debriefs with such grace, it feels effortless, and learners hardly even notice until it's already happened. In reality, we go to great lengths to ensure each aspect of the experience flows smoothly. Each program is unique, and so too are the logistical considerations. However, there are a few key categories to help you prepare:

- **Test technology.** In a post-pandemic world, after virtual training took center stage for much of 2020–2021, testing our technology has become second nature for many. If you are running a virtual training or will use technology in the physical classroom, figure out what your tech check might involve. For example, can learners test their ability to connect to a virtual platform before arriving for training? If your program asks learners to bring their own device, what will you do if someone doesn't bring their device to ensure the learning experience is equitable? Planning for potential what-ifs is key to success.

- **Have multiple back-up plans.** Preparing to facilitate is the time to ask ourselves, "What if this doesn't work?" We need to consider what we will do if technology fails, an activity falls flat, or our learners follow a different path than we predicted. Consider having at least two or three back-up plans for all major activities and exercises in your program. If the intention of a given activity is to support learning, how will you ensure learning takes place if the activity fails?

- **Create space for mental presence.** We need to plan to give ourselves time to be present and maintain a state of presence. How can you take other tasks, priorities, and distractions off your plate to be fully in the learning experience with and for your learners?

- **Checklists.** Create checklists for anything and everything you might need (a great example of holding yourself able). This includes a materials checklist listing wall charts, other teaching aids, and materials for activities, like playing cards, or markers. Technology checklists help ensure you've prepared everything ahead of time to test out potential challenges, such as extra USB cords for computer setup, a clicker to advance your slides, and a test of the internet connection and of any videos that may be a part of the program. If you are concerned about responsibilities falling through the cracks, capture them on a checklist to be reviewed prior to each delivery. Checklists are your deep breaths. So, you can never have too many.

One resource we use on the ATD facilitator team is a checklist that helps guide our considerations and preparations. Each facilitator can use this checklist to customize to their own style and priorities as needed. See the following checklist for the face-to-face classroom. When you're done reviewing, consider using this template to build a checklist for your virtual classroom environment.

[Program Name] Materials and Setup Checklist

Face-to-Face Classroom Preparation Materials
- Pre-work (for reference)
- Timing guide (for reference)
  - Sorting methods listed by each activity for quick reference
- Candy/prizes
- Sticky notes (one pad per participant)
- Markers for wall charts
- Bluetooth speaker (as needed)
- USB cables for projection
- Wireless clicker (with extra batteries)
- Hand sanitizer
- Test polling software
- Wi-Fi and polling code written on wall chart

Day 1
Standard Wall Charts
- Welcome! Facilitator information listed, Wi-Fi code, poll codes
- Course learning objectives
- What's in it for me (WIIFM)
- Agenda, one for each day (optional)
- Parking lot (optional)
- Training cycle
- Wows? (+) How Abouts? (-)
  - To collect Level 1 feedback at the end of each day
- Resource center (for resources and further study from peers)

Activities Materials and Setup
- Activity wall charts
  - (list all activities by title, materials needed)

- Evaluation Concept Center activity
  - Table tents labeled center 1, 2, 3 (2 sets)
  - Sticky notes with words from the word bank
  - Envelopes to hold directions
  - Paper with the instructions *and* discussion question printed out for each station

How Do I Prepare *Myself?*

Being present for our learners means we want to minimize as much as possible any noise from our brains or lives, so it doesn't interfere with what we do with learners in the classroom. That does not mean we should ignore ourselves; in fact, it's quite the opposite. It means we need to pay attention to our needs before they interfere with our facilitation. Within the context of training, Abraham Maslow's Hierarchy of Needs (Figure 2-1) is most often used to better consider the needs of our learners. It can also be applied to facilitators as we prepare for a delivery.

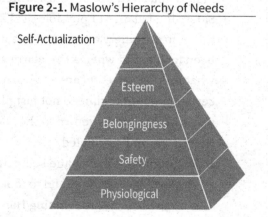

Figure 2-1. Maslow's Hierarchy of Needs

Self-Actualization

Esteem

Belongingness

Safety

Physiological

The model contends that people have complex needs that they strive to fulfill, and that those needs change and evolve (Maslow 1943). Individuals achieve the next level of the hierarchy only after lower-level needs have been satisfied. Maslow categorized these needs into a logical hierarchy from physiological to psychological:

- **Physiological needs** include food, drink, and sleep.
- **Safety** needs include freedom from fear and the need to be safe and stable.
- **Belongingness** is the need for friends and family.

- **Esteem** includes self-esteem and the need to be highly regarded by others.
- **Self-actualization** is the need to excel.

In essence, we need to be very aware of our own needs and how we can satisfy them to effectively show up for our learners.

- **Physiological needs** are the first, or lowest, level in the hierarchy and therefore demand the most immediate attention. Paying attention to physiological needs is important because they override or negatively impact any higher-level needs when they are ignored or not taken care of. Simple yet consistent considerations like eating balanced meals, exercising, and getting a good night's sleep before a delivery can make all the difference in how you show up for your learners.
- **Safety** is a balance of physiological and psychological needs. A threat to our safety can trigger a fear response. If you have ever been facilitating when a fire alarm starts blaring, you know what this feels like. It can take learners, and sometimes us, a certain amount of time to not just physically respond to the alarm, but mentally return to the learning environment after the fire alarm has quieted.
- **Belongingness, esteem, and self-actualization,** the higher levels of Maslow's hierarchy, attend to more psychological needs. As Susan David, an award-winning Harvard Medical School psychologist, said in a 2017 TED Talk, "Emotions are data; they are not directives." The same is true of our emotions being tied to specific needs.

As we prepare to facilitate a new program for the first time, we may be challenged by a lack of confidence or belongingness due to what has so aptly been deemed *impostor syndrome* on social media feeds and industry blogs. Imposter syndrome is defined as "a psychological pattern in which an individual doubts their skills, talents, or accomplishments and has a persistent internalized fear of being exposed as a 'fraud'" (Langford 1993).

This thought process is driven by the fear that your esteem needs will not be met if you make a mistake during the delivery. Your content and logistical preparation can support you here, because you should already have a plan in place if something goes wrong or does not work the way you intended. Additionally, ask yourself what you are afraid of and what you need to overcome the fear to begin questioning your needs and evaluate your emotions as data. Let's use the definition of *imposter syndrome* to do some truth-telling. Use Table 2-1 to document your skills, talents, and accomplishments as they pertain to facilitation and training delivery. Capture every detail. We gave you one of our own examples to start your thinking. The next time that self-doubt creeps in, be sure to conduct your reality check against the list you've generated of who you are and what you're capable of.

Table 2-1. Listing Your Strengths

Skills	Talents	Accomplishments
Building on learner comments	Links previous questions to current content and re-establishes relevance for learners	Helping learners tie the content together and link questions to examples given elsewhere in the program, resulting in increased retention

How Do You Protect (or Find) Preparation Time?

We have a hard and fast rule on our facilitation team at ATD: Protect your prep! This means blocking an hour of time on each end of training delivery for preparation and reflection. For a delivery on new content, this could mean blocking days prior and treating preparation time as an essential meeting that can't be skipped. Setting clear boundaries, for yourself and others, around preparation is key to your success. To get started in protecting your own preparation time, identify what you need to be successful and ask for alignment from your team and supervisor.

The preparation process is how we succeed as facilitators. The time spent here is just as important as the time spent in the classroom. It may take additional effort from us to alert our colleagues, friends, and family to the importance of this time and get their alignment on helping us protect the preparation process.

An established routine that prepares you for the first minute of your facilitation can be very helpful. Engaging regular activities that satisfy your needs and preparation will signal both your conscious and subconscious mind about what is to come: facilitation. If your preparation routine takes a day, attach that to the beginning of every learning event.

Also recognize that despite our best efforts, we will at some point encounter the need to condense our preparation time. In fact, that is more often our reality than not. In these instances, what are the things you absolutely need to be successful in your preparation time? How can you prioritize the need-to-haves and release the nice-to-haves in your routine? Even if you do not have full control of your schedule, find small ways to work your routine into what you are doing each day. Let's look at some of our specific processes as an example.

Facilitation in Action

Preparing for the Face-to-Face Classroom

When learners ask Carrie how she established confidence in her facilitation, one of the key things she returns to is preparation. The two are directly correlated, and her impact is lessened or strengthened depending on the amount of preparation she does. When preparing for the face-to-face classroom, her process is quite involved:

1. Collect and review all the materials that contribute to the learning (facilitator guide, participant workbook or guide, PowerPoint slides, handouts, videos, a recording of an audit of a similar program, and the organizational goals and original training request).

2. Begin with the visuals of the course design. Carrie is a visual learner and will click through a PowerPoint deck for comprehension of what she's teaching and in what order to build mental models of the course flow. Then she clicks through at least two more times to get a sense of pace and flow of the program. The visual review of the slides helps create triggers that are easier for her to remember in the moment of facilitation.

3. Use the facilitator guide and participant workbook or guide in tandem. Carrie wants to see what her prompts are in direct association with what the learner sees. It allows her to compare the-behind-the-curtain view (facilitator guide) with what's in front of the curtain (participant-facing materials).

4. Read the facilitator guide front to back, out loud. That last part is important. Vocalizing allows her to practice delivering the content in her own style, tone, and pace. Moving through it aloud as a rehearsal also intuitively helps her identify moments where an example, an anecdote, or a story might amplify the learning. It helps her find moments for questions or silence to enable deeper thinking. She marks these moments in the facilitator guide in all caps for ease of reference in the moment of facilitation (such as PODCAST STORY, GIRAFFE STORY, or ORGANIZATIONAL ASSESSMENT STORY).

5. For every activity on the timing sheet, write the sorting method to quickly and clearly provide a variety of engagement techniques to sort participants. For example:

    Exercise 1.3: Preparing to Facilitate—Groups of 4, group by favorite season.

6. Link content together or link it to outcomes and objectives to improve flow and transition. To do this, Carrie maps her facilitator guide. For each lesson she writes a few words in the margin with what the takeaway should be for the learner. For each module she links those words from each lesson together and writes out transitions into the next topic areas. When she performs this activity, the learners can make those connections quicker as well.

7. Do a full rehearsal (including standing and leveraging movement). Carrie will rehearse several times until the moment she begins to get comfortable stepping away from the facilitator guide and moving through the content on her own. She knows she's ready when she can begin imagining learners engaging with certain points and pose questions to herself to challenge her own responses. She rehearses the first five minutes of a program several times because she knows that for her, these moments define the energy for the rest of the delivery.

To compress the above preparation to accommodate reduced timelines, identify the two things that have the biggest impact on the learner (not you) and start there. For Carrie, that's numbers 2 and 6.

On the day of the training, Carrie is a firm believer in setting a clear intention for the program. What does she want to use as a guide to center herself throughout the training? Maybe it's "have fun" or "aim for impact" or "leverage learner stories."

Facilitation in Action

Preparing for the Virtual Classroom

Similar to Carrie's process, Nikki finds it essential to prepare the task-heavy environment of the virtual classroom with a process that helps her focus on the learner more than the content:

1. Print out the timing chart. Nikki writes in her time zone and the minutes she "should" be starting each lesson/topic. This helps her adapt when timing gets off track. She adds this to her bulletin

board so that she can quickly glance at it when she needs to during the virtual session.

2. Highlight potential areas to trim down or cut out if needed to make up time to allow for on-the-fly adjustments. Nikki also communicates these to the producer ahead of time to ensure the flow is not compromised.

3. Read through the entire facilitator guide and add relevant stories and examples to bring it to life. Nikki also reads through the participant guide to understand what learners will be experiencing. She reviews her slides and practices moving through and advancing as she would on the day of the session.

4. As time permits, do a complete run-through of the entire program to practice timing and flow, and to continue familiarizing herself with what's next. This allows Nikki to flex in the moment of facilitation to the learners' needs as they arise during the course. This also includes testing the features of the virtual platform.

5. Most important, test the technology and review any videos, podcasts, and demos thoroughly. This includes writing out personal notes about each learner to be able to reference them when interacting during the session. She also checks her setup to ensure her desk is prepared to aid in facilitation, not detract from it.

What's Next?

As we have learned from this chapter, there is no single right way to prepare ourselves for facilitating learning. Our unique facilitation style will influence how we prepare. On our team, we aim to create checklists, clear expectations, and guidance, while also allowing the space for each facilitator to define a process that suits their personality and style. This also helps facilitators create consistency in training delivery while still allowing the uniqueness of each facilitator to shine.

Invitation

Consider the following questions to identify or establish your preparation routine. Try answering the questions that jump off the page at you first.

1. What could you do more of to set the stage for your training programs?
    _____
    _____

2. What are you currently doing to prepare for facilitation?
    _____
    _____

3. Using the answers from the previous questions, which two items do you feel most effectively prepare you to facilitate?
    _____
    _____

4. What are two new practices (things you have not done, or have not done regularly) you would like to add to your preparation routine?
    _____
    _____

5. Consider documenting your preparation process for each modality you facilitate in (virtual, in-person). Once you have dictated the process, try establishing an approximate time to associate with that preparation process and begin communicating that to team members.
    _____
    _____

Chapter 3
Your Role in Learning

Understanding your unique role in the overall success of talent development within your organization and even more broadly in the field is essential. So, this leads to the question: What is the facilitator's role in learning?

A 2020 ATD research report, *Effective Trainers: Traditional and Virtual Classroom Success,* surveyed more than 450 talent development professionals to examine the roles and knowledge of trainers, as well as the strategies and tools used for delivering training. In the report, 40 percent of those surveyed were solely dedicated to training delivery. The majority, which made up the remaining 60 percent of respondents, spread their time and contributions across content development and design, program and project management, on-the-job coaching and learning reinforcement, evaluating impact, and the nebulous category of "other."

As the survey data tells us, TD professionals are involved in multiple facets of the L&D function, and we've broadened our reach and influence into project management, strategic programs, and business acumen. It's not enough to facilitate learning; trainers and facilitators also have the added responsibility of linking learning priorities to the strategic direction of the organization.

The Role of the Facilitator

With many facilitators wearing multiple hats, the role is not as clearly defined as it once was. Some facilitators serve as double agents donning the hat of instructional designer and facilitator, both creating and implementing learning programs. While we honor that reality (and provide some tips for performance later in this chapter), for the purposes of this book, we'll focus solely on the role of the trainer or facilitator. Our role, then, has two central components:

- **Create the space and experience to enable learning.** The first is all about the physical or virtual space, the in-person classroom (meeting room, rental facility, or corporate venue) or the platform (WebEx, Adobe Connect, Microsoft Teams, or Zoom) that houses your course experience. In short, the literal space where the training is taking place. This also includes the intangible environment we create as facilitators. The intangibles include how we connect with learners, how we build rapport, how we develop relationships among learners to encourage peer-based collaboration. We are the caretakers of not just where learning takes place, but also how it takes place.

- **Create the opportunity for learning to improve workplace performance.** This is all about training serving as a mechanism to change behavior and improve performance. The design of a training is guided by learning objectives and business outcomes, and so is our delivery of that training. It's our responsibility to provide learners the opportunity to learn and successfully achieve the anticipated outcomes of the training. We need to ensure our learners are gaining value in some way from the experience and can immediately apply new skills and knowledge back on the job. This speaks more directly to why learning takes place.

For Your Consideration

What Do We Call the Space Where Learning Takes Place?
Great question! It depends.

Even as we came together to write this book, we found ourselves toggling between mentions of *class*, *classroom*, *event*, *program*, and *experience* to properly refer to workplace learning. All these terms accurately refer to the place where learning happens, each with its own subtle nuances. The key is to ensure your team and organization are aligned and everyone is speaking the same language. Ultimately, we as ATD facilitators most often use *learning experience* because it encapsulates not only the main event but the elements that occur before, during, and after a training to define the systems approach that leads to performance improvement.

The learning experience encompasses the modalities, the physical environment, the group dynamics, the materials, the design, the media used, the activities deployed, digital assets, hybrid models, facilitators, and learners. Each of these valuable and necessary components weaves together to form the overall learning experience.

The Talent Development Capability Model identifies capabilities across three domains—individual, professional, and organizational—to provide a blueprint for the TD professional to grow and become more effective. As training delivery professionals, we of course need to hone our skills in that professional space, but our role can and should reach across the organization and encompass organizational capabilities like consulting, business partnering, change management, business insight, and future readiness, as well as individual capabilities like lifelong learning, emotional intelligence, decision making, and cultural awareness and inclusion.

What If I'm a Department of One and Serving in a Lot of Different Roles?

First, let's establish the reality: You are not a superhero. You don't have a cape to throw across your shoulders in moments when you need super-human strength and abilities to get the job done (unless you do, in which case, we'd like to meet you). So where do you start? You start by being realistic with yourself and your stakeholders.

Learning and development practitioners need to be able to recognize what their strengths are, when they will require extra time to learn how to accomplish a task, and when they may have to reach out to others for help. The biggest constraint in this situation is typically time. We often hear from learners in our ATD programs, "Everything you've taught is extremely helpful and on target, but I'm only one person. There's no way I can do all this." We get it—we've been there. We are there.

Following are some tips we often pass along to learners who face this challenge (adapted from O'Keeffe 2020a). Adhering to these practices can keep you on an even keel, preventing burnout.

Make Each Project Step Micro

When you're crunched for time, instead of skipping a step altogether, do a mini needs assessment. Rather than not asking any questions when starting a learning project, ask one or two. They could be along the lines of "Why do we need this?" or "What is the business outcome we hope to accomplish from this request?"

Be Realistic About Time Commitments

When we're asked to develop learning solutions or deliver them, our first thought may be, "Yes, I can do that in a month." But remember that many projects take longer than you expect and that you may get pulled off one project for another that is a higher strategic priority. So, give yourself and your client a longer timeframe than you think you'll need and be prepared to negotiate.

One tool for negotiation and expectation setting we share in our ATD programs is to leverage the industry research that details how long it takes to develop one hour of training (Defelice 2021). When a stakeholder asks for a live online learning solution to be implemented in 30 days, consider using the research presented in Table 3-1 as you negotiate for more time. Here's what that might sound like: "I understand the business needs of your request and want to support the rapid development of the program. I also want to ensure I'm providing you with the expertise from a development perspective so we can plan together to ensure we meet the organization's goals. Did you know, for instance, that research shows the average time to develop a live online synchronous program is 55 hours for every one hour of instruction? For the requested three-day program, you're looking at 1,320 hours of development time. If we can't plan the project around the suggested development hours, is there a way we could work together to find a more achievable timeline?"

Table 3-1. How Long It Takes to Develop Instruction

Modality	Average Time to Develop One Hour of Instruction (Hours)
In-person instructor-led classroom	67
Live online or virtual instructor-led classroom	55
Asynchronous e-learning	155
Microlearning assets	18

Adapted from Defelice (2021).

While you can't always expect to receive the amount of time research provides, it does help paint a picture of an ideal time allotment and help you gain more time than the initial request. A typical follow-up response to this approach we hear in our programs is, "I'm not comfortable having those conversations." To that, we often remind the trainers and facilitators in our train-the-trainer programs, your role is not limited to your training delivery. You are in fact an integral part of the talent development machine, and consulting and partnering with key stakeholders to offer your expertise to guide their projects is an essential skill.

Understand How Much Your Time Is Worth

You need to acknowledge that you're not going to be adept at everything. Perhaps you've never done any e-learning. Or you lack experience with video. Maybe now is not the time to start. How many hours will it take you to get up to speed? Can you buy a module on the training topic instead of building it? Conduct a cost-benefit analysis on either the project as a whole or certain aspects of initiatives. Are you the best person to be doing the work? Or would it be more cost effective to outsource it? Can someone else internally conduct a data analysis? Know your strengths and capabilities and plan accordingly.

Try One New Thing

It's easy to want to make use of all the new information and tools immediately. Instead, we suggest you choose one tool, technique, or application to begin incorporating into your next training, then build on that success when you're comfortable with the first tool. It's a marathon, not a sprint.

Leverage Subject Matter Experts (SMEs)

Ensuring that course content is kept current can be overwhelming if you're doing it on your own. Our general rule is to review materials on a quarterly basis. Start that review process by asking the subject matter expert to look over the curriculum for necessary changes. A pro tip is to develop a process whereby SMEs make changes to the materials to save you time. After the SMEs are finished with their review, manage the rollout.

For Your Consideration

Setting Expectations

You can't facilitate every class. You can't design every class. You can't coordinate every class. So, what can you do and whom can you leverage as a partner? In a previous role, Darryl approached a learning partner and asked for some assistance. The colleague explained, "I spend about 5 percent of my time thinking about training. I have a list of other things I'm doing." Darryl had to respect the clear boundaries that were established by that colleague, and with that information the two were able to set expectations for their interactions in a way that supported his co-worker and were still respectful of his own schedule and primary duties.

Leverage the business. Find individuals in your business who are passionate about developing people. Jared has been lucky enough in previous companies that mid- to senior-level managers were passionate about developing people. He leveraged their passions and energy as SMEs for their manager training program, and built a community of local learning ambassadors to aid in the development process. He became adept at constantly advocating to others for what he did and how he could help them, and then asking for what he needed from them.

Get scrappy. In initiatives where resources (time, budget, people, belief) run short, Carrie creates a grassroots effort to leverage what she does have at the time. Identify champions of your effort to help influence others around your ask. For years, Carrie was a single person responsible for the business growth, sales, and education of a bi-state territory. She had to get comfortable with asking others for their partnership to reach a business outcome. Her approach was to create a vision of what the project would look like at completion and communicate that vision and the impacts that effort would have to her partners. Then, she would state what her needs were and ask for their partnership in one of those key areas.

How Do I Create a Safe and Positive Learning Environment?

Think of one of the best experiences you have had as a learner. Transport yourself back to that specific place and time and try to recall what made the experience so great. What made it beneficial? Now, think about the environment and describe every detail. What was on the walls or the table you sat at? What was your relationship with the facilitator and fellow learners? Move through your five senses to describe this experience. What did you see the facilitator do to create the environment that you still remember today?

We do not have absolute control over our learning spaces, but there are a lot of choices and considerations we can make to support the creation of a positive learning environment. Safety has taken on an entirely new meaning in a post-pandemic world, especially in training environments. But the question remains, how do we create a safe, comfortable, and positive learning environment, especially when the needs of individual learners vary greatly?

Model the Right Behaviors

Building a positive learning environment is core to the facilitator's role and aids in creating relevance and buy-in for our learners. Through behavior modeling, based on social learning theory, you are inviting learners to observe your engagement, questioning, and vulnerability to create a level of safety for learners to fully contribute. For Darryl, this effort starts with modeling the same behaviors he's trying to cultivate in his programs. When he's teaching ATD's Training & Facilitation Certificate or Master Trainer program, for instance, his facilitation is a blueprint of the expectations of a Master Trainer. Not only will he discuss the topic of overcoming challenging behaviors and situations, but he will model what he teaches when a challenge arises in the flow of the program.

Meet Learner Needs

This all links back to Maslow's Hierarchy of Needs, which we covered in chapter 2. If you're worried about the lower rungs on Maslow's hierarchy (physiological, safety, belongingness), nothing on a higher level (like knowledge acquisition) will happen. As a facilitator, Jared thinks of what he can do to help learners meet those needs or to build parameters, guidelines, and structures that allow for safety, belonging, and esteem to build a learner toward achieving their optimum potential during the training.

Establish Group Commitments

One often overlooked and underutilized approach is the use of group commitments (also referred to as best practices or ground rules). Rather than creating a list of guidelines for the adult learners in your program to adhere to, involve them in setting the parameters. The ATD facilitator team has a method for establishing group commitments in an inclusive way. We start with a wall chart or virtual whiteboard titled Group Commitments and pose a question like this: "Let's begin with a conversation around how we best want to learn together and identify some commitments we will make to ourselves, to our group, and to the learning. What do you need from each other to have an ideal learning experience?" Then we populate the suggestions on the wall chart. If time permits, follow up with, "What do you need from me?" and "What do you need from yourself?" Once the list is compiled, place it somewhere in the physical space for the duration of the program. Because the learners have contributed to the list, they will be more likely to adhere to it. Adult learning theory tells us adults are self-motivated, so aid them in that through this exercise.

Connect the People

The facilitator's role is ever changing. Nikki now asks questions about how the learners and she can show up for one another and collectively build a safe and comfortable environment. Once she connects people and establishes parameters for how they can best work with one another, they can get down to the business of learning together. She does this with approaches like group commitments, setting a pace-checker system to ensure learners feel comfortable sharing if the pace is too fast or too slow, and most important, leveraging various icebreakers, energizers, and discussions to foster community in her learning events.

Normalize Mistakes

Establishing and maintaining a positive learning environment is a human-centered and service-minded process. Carrie spends a lot of energy not only creating that environment but modeling it. She wants to normalize mistakes in her learning spaces so participants can learn to muck it up and create a space where there is freedom to fail. She wants to normalize feelings in a training program and allow the learners to dictate what they need to be successful, which allows them to be a part of creating that space instead of having it dictated to them. Ultimately, it's not about defining what makes a safe environment for the learners. It's about helping them define it for themselves, and turn it into guidelines that shape the learning experience.

To normalize mistakes, Carrie is quick to model for learners identifying what went wrong and how it could have been better in train-the-trainer programs to support the analysis of the training delivery. When she provides instructions prior to an activity and receives blank stares or delayed action, she knows that something in her phrasing must have caused confusion. Rather than proceed with confusion, Carrie pauses and says, "Well that didn't make much sense, did it. Would it be helpful for me to try again?" This approach not only provides clarity but models vulnerability, and in a train-the-trainer program, that can be a key takeaway.

How Do I Scale My Delivery for Varying Participant Sizes?

We see this question a lot in our ATD facilitation sessions. Our role as facilitator can quickly shift from a one-on-one coaching scenario to a facilitated workshop for 200 or more attendees. How do you scale your delivery for varying audience sizes? At the root of this question is another: How do you pivot? Here are some tips.

Focus on Adaptation and Leverage Technology and Tools

Facilitators can adapt for the size of the audience by leveraging technology and focusing on how activities and outcomes can be achieved through different methods. As the size of her group grows, Nikki knows she can't give as many personal touchpoints as often as she'd like, including inviting round-robin responses to questions or stories and examples from each member of the group. Instead, she leverages technology to allow for voice and interaction points using tools like Slido, Quizlet, and Mentimeter.

Create Opportunities for Connection

While we can't partner up a group of 150 learners in the same way we would a group of 20, we can have them stay seated and turn to a neighbor to discuss a topic. This allows the connection to occur while adapting to the limitations of space and audience size. Another technique is asking those with experience in a certain skill, topic area, or industry to stand, and then inviting those seated to identify someone standing with whom they want to engage in a conversation on the next break or for an upcoming activity. For virtual sessions, consider leveraging webcams intentionally at key moments of collaboration as opposed to having them on throughout the program.

Adjust Methods and Activities

Focus on what you do have instead of what you don't have. Small-group activities are not as effective an instructional method in large audiences, but leveraging the layout is a great approach. For instance, using the sides of the room, four corners of the room, rows of seats, or stickers on the arms of chairs are great ways to leverage the space to conduct activities. Carrie always aims to make space for connection to enable other learners to help one another draw connections. Focus on big ideas to encode into memory through peer-to-peer connection.

What's My Role Once the Training Is Over?

On our facilitator team at ATD, we subscribe to the notion that our role never truly ends. Sure, an instance or event concludes, but your role and involvement in facilitating an experience that impacts performance back on the job doesn't ever end. Be it through ongoing performance support, follow-up training programs, or mentoring and coaching programs within your organization, your impact is not reduced to a single event. Post-training activities, like mentoring and coaching, ensure retention and application back on the job.

When measuring the effectiveness of learning solutions, we use Donald Kirkpatrick's Four Levels of Evaluation and Jack Phillips's added Level 5 to assess learning programs. The model allows for both formative and summative feedback, and one of the most impactful activities we facilitate in our training delivery programs is around how to measure at each of the levels. Evaluation can help you begin to understand what your role as a facilitator is before, during, and even after training (Table 3-2). In particular, look at the levels of impact that occur after the learning event is done, and think about *how* you can extend your influence to these.

Table 3-2. Levels of Evaluation

Level 1: Reaction—Did they like it?
• End of day feedback forms (smile sheets) • Wow/How About wall chart (where learners place feedback around "wows" and feedback with suggestions for shifting in the remainder of the program under "how abouts") • Keep/start/stop • Surveys or polling (using apps like Slido or Mentimeter)
Level 2: Learning—Did they learn it (within the confines of the course)?
• Tests and quizzes • Skills practice and role play • Demonstrations • Teach-backs • Case studies or scenarios • Simulations
Level 3: Behavior—Did they apply it (back on the job)?
• Work observation of procedure or end product • Ride-alongs (for field-based employees) • Focus groups • On-the-job coaching
Level 4: Results—Did they impact the business?
• Sales • Expenses • Error rates • Retention rates • Absenteeism
Level 5: ROI—Did the training generate a return on the investment?
• ROI calculations • Months to years to complete • Stat analysis • Cost-benefit analysis

ATD's 2019 research report *Effective Evaluation* found that of the talent development professionals surveyed, 88 percent were measuring at Level 1, with 80 percent measuring at Level 2. At higher levels, the numbers reduce considerably: 60 percent when measuring Level 3, 35 percent measuring Level 4, and 15 percent measuring Level 5. Four percent of respondents were not measuring the effectiveness of training solutions at all. The report reflected the trends in the industry and highlighted the reality that some trainers and facilitators will not have access to the data required to move into Levels 3–5.

Additionally, you'll sometimes find yourself without the formal structure or organizational (even departmental) support to allow you to supplement your training with additional resources, workshops, or coaching. To that end, we've collected a few approaches to ensure your training efforts don't stop the moment the last learner logs offline or walks out of your classroom.

- **Empowerment.** Leverage an activity or a debrief in the training itself to help connect learners to resources, people, and approaches to enable them to apply what they've learned when they are back on the job. For example, at the end of the training, post a wall chart that lists five or six brief scenarios (barriers) that could occur when they are back on the job. Have the group work in self-selected pairs to document ways to overcome that barrier if it occurs. This helps learners action plan how they can anticipate and solve for challenges that may occur and empowers them to take action they need to successfully perform.
- **Support.** Determine how you can support learners post-training. Provide your preferred method, time, and topics to reconnect on post-training. Set up 30-day check-ins where you reach out to learners post-training with a specific question. Rather than, "How are things going for you since our training?" be specific and ask, "How are those five steps to conflict management working out for you as you practice with your team? What barriers have you encountered?" The more specific your questions, the more support you can truly provide.
- **Ownership of learning.** This relates back to our conversation on holding our learners able rather than accountable. If we've

empowered them to apply what they've learned and supported them with supplemental resources and conversations, the learner will ideally begin reaching out to peers, referencing course materials, even asking for someone to observe a process and provide feedback. As facilitators, we can have a large impact on teaching them how to take ownership of their learning.

- **Follow up as promised or required.** Did you promise to provide a resource, an industry article, or more details on a process? If you used the phrase "I'll follow up" or used a parking lot to collect items, questions, and comments that you would follow up on later, then do just that. And quickly.

Facilitation in Action

A Powerful Close

The close is also about empowerment. For Jared, this means a role shift from facilitation and leading learners through an experience to enabling them to become the driver of their learning and application. When working with mid-level managers during a leadership development program, Jared led learners through two days of content, activities, and conversations. They actively developed an understanding of their styles and approaches to their teams, and once they left the workshop they were prepared to implement new skills and knowledge back on the job. Jared supported this effort through informal check-ins with each leader as they implemented their approaches into their day-to-day offering by providing resources and coaching and connecting them to other leaders for continued support. "As facilitators, we take temporary ownership of participants' development to guide them through the learning. At the conclusion of the training, the ownership transfers back to them and the practical application of our trainings aims to prepare them for that transition. We can join them, of course, if they invite us, but the control remains with them."

When Darryl first started as a facilitator, the types of programs he facilitated were two-week courses with a single cohort of learners. If they passed the class, they got the job they were training for, so this was a high-reward training program. Working with learners for two weeks, he developed relationships with learners and got to know them. After the training he shifted from facilitator and leader to colleague and resource. He had a 130-person network of trainees. He would drive around to see those he'd trained, and it gave him insight on the impact of the training. When he doesn't have that same opportunity to track progress, he leverages technology and social platforms to honor that promise he made in the training to support their development.

When Carrie conducted field sales and management training, she noticed a reoccurring trend. Her learners came together two times a month for education sessions, one focused on product and one focused on service. Working with these learners consistently built trust and rapport and Carrie leveraged her practical and down-to-earth style to keep engagement high. However, the service trainings were plagued by the same response from her learners: "This is great in the training but in my day-to-day, it's harder to use." Seeing that her learners had the knowledge and demonstrated the skills in the training, she recognized the challenge was in recalling on the job and applying what they'd learned. Carrie quickly pivoted her approach to include a work observation process where she shadowed job performance immediately after the service training, providing on-the-job coaching. This also allowed her to recognize the barriers and tailor future trainings to overcome those barriers. Additionally, she worked with the management team to tailor its team-based messages via mobile updates to also include a brief tip or check-in regarding that month's service topic, so the training was infused into other methods of communication outside the expected training dates.

What's Next?

Continue asking yourself the question this chapter poses: What is the role of the facilitator in learning? Its beauty is that it's constantly evolving, shaped by the individuals we train, the organizations we work for or with, and the communities that our efforts impact.

As facilitators, we have a direct impact on how someone shows up in their day-to-day lives at work and, sometimes if we're lucky enough, how they show up personally as well. Our role is not only about what we do for our learners but about what we do in preparing to engage with others. Our role in learning is equal parts what we ourselves learn and what we enable others to learn.

Invitation

Let's do a little vision work as you reflect on your role.

1. Define your why. Why do you do what you do?

   _____

   _____

2. Write out a personal mantra or tagline that supports your why. (It should be easy to recall when needed.)

   _____

   _____

3. Draw, doodle, or create a hashtag or emoticon to visually represent your role as a facilitator.

   _____

   _____

Consider these questions to reflect on how you will continue to define your role in learning.

1. Who is the modern learner? (If you're not sure, begin with Josh Bersin's "Meet the Modern Learner" infographic and consider how you'd update it to align to learners today. And also, check out Bersin's latest *HR Predictions* report.

   _____

   _____

2. When will you create a learning experience versus a learning event? Why?

   _____

   _____

3. What one new technique will you try in order to create a safe environment for your learners?

   _____

   _____

4. Are you a department of one? If so, how do you gain support? Are you on a team? If so, how can you strengthen those partnerships?

   _____

   _____

Chapter 4
Developing Your Style

Whether you're talking about your fashion sense, your home décor, your communication style, or the *New York Times* style section, one thing remains constant. Style is rooted in observation. The benefit: When you're clear about your facilitation style, you are better prepared in a moment of need. ATD recognizes that every facilitator has a personal preference when it comes to their style of training delivery and expects facilitators to adapt to meet the needs and varying preferences of the learners.

You know you've cultivated a facilitation style when you begin to see common words or phrases in feedback from your colleagues like "I love attending your sessions because they are so practical and down-to-earth," or evaluation feedback deems you "humorous, kind, and empathetic." That feedback is giving you information on how others perceive your style and can be a great indicator of what you need to cultivate and continue to develop.

When we think of facilitation styles, those we have observed as learners ourselves or those we have observed from mentors or peers, we can begin to generate an exhaustive list of adjectives: *service-minded, people-focused, practical, funny, empathic, down-to-earth, learner-centered, focused,* or *firm,* to name a few.

Style is study-able and shapeable. As facilitators we should aim to be ongoing students of style by observing colleagues and peers, attending industry conferences to see a variety of styles in action, and recording training sessions at our organizations for peer-based review and critique sessions. Doing this will help us create an inventory of characteristics around facilitation styles we admire.

What Training Delivery Skills Are Central to Developing My Style?

In short, several. Imagine this: You are facilitating at a financial organization to a group of 20 customer care representatives with varying experience levels on the topic of enhanced customer service. The goal of the annual training is to realign to organizational policy and procedures and train around core concerns revealed in recent customer survey data. The program's design includes a teach-back activity where you divide and conquer the content that is dense and not engaging (as tends to be the case with "policy and procedure" training). You instruct each group to review the material, become the expert in the content area they have been assigned, and prepare an eight-minute teach-back for the rest of the learners that illustrates key points of the content. When you observe the teach-back portion, you quickly realize that the activity was not effective because the first group of learners teaching back to the larger group are sharing information that is not going to get the other learners to reach the intended learning objectives. Their teach-backs (intended to be eight minutes) are more like two to three minutes at most and are not covering key points but generally stating the areas of the content that they connected to.

What do you do to resolve this challenge? How does your training style shine through in this moment? What skills do you lean on to get the group back on course? Depending on your facilitation style, there are a variety of options. As you read below, circle (yes, we believe in marking up books a good bit) the facilitation skills that you see exhibited in each approach.

Collaborative

Jared's style is to ask more questions of the learners so the collective "we" in the training is reaching the outcome. This sounds like, "How did your team reach that result? Were there any challenges in reaching that result?" rather than, "That is not quite right . . . here is what I was looking for." His style is to dig into the different approaches and let different people learn from one another. The style you have allows you to choose specific training skills from your toolbox to emulate that style. In this case, Jared's collaborative style has him choose an approach of asking questions rooted in importance and process to take the learners deeper.

Adaptable

Darryl goes into all his classes with a mindset and willingness to make changes when necessary to fit the needs of the learners. In this scenario, as soon as he discovers the overall group is missing the mark, he would start to run through the options he has available to help get the learners back on track while they continue with their teach-backs. This requires him to make a quick decision in real time, and he typically chooses to follow his instincts when deciding to switch things up. He'd ask himself, "Do I have enough time to model an example to the group?" "Do I need to give the group an additional small exercise to allow an opportunity to gain deeper understanding of the topic?" and "Can I leverage the experienced learners to help fill in the knowledge gaps?"

Learner-Centric

Nikki's first question to the group when she sees they are off track is, "How was that experience for you?" rather than, "Tell us more about point number 4 of the policy, because it is still unclear." By asking how the experience was, she may uncover that learners did not understand the activity instructions, or they did not have enough time, resources, or experience to complete the activity. When she has that information, then she can determine where to head next. Next may be working on the content together as a large group, leveraging experts in the room on the content piece, or the facilitator asking permission to fill in the gaps. Nikki would then conclude with, "If we were to try a teach-back activity like this again in the future, what could we do differently to make it more successful?"

Integrity

As a facilitator whose style is rooted in being service-minded, Carrie accepts the responsibility for the activity not reaching the desired outcome. Perhaps she could have provided more guidance up front when providing instructions for the activity or provided an example of what a good teach-back looks like to set learners up for success. In this case, the activity didn't achieve its stated objective, ultimately leaving the learners no better off than when they started. She might spend extra time in the debrief helping them fill in the gaps while adding additional context. For instance, "When it comes to point number 2 of our policy, I imagine there might be challenges to consider. What might we want to consider? Let's build a list together." What feels like a standard debrief is designed to use content-specific questions to tease out the information from the participants that will help them meet the objective. Then, because the instructional method of the teach-back didn't initially succeed, she'd conclude the debrief by asking, "Now that we've done a teach-back, how would you approach this activity differently as a learner next time?" This allows them to reflect on what went well and what didn't.

You can see some similarities and differences in our responses based on our varying facilitation styles. Perhaps most important, you see there isn't just one right way to facilitate. There are multiple approaches to take given the variety of skill sets we have in our toolbox. Ensuring your responses align to your facilitation style allows you to facilitate with confidence, authenticity, and intention.

How Do I Build My Confidence in Facilitation?

By the very nature of our role as trainers and facilitators, we show up every day for a role that ends with people evaluating us, rating just how successful (or unsuccessful) we were—even telling us if they (gulp!) liked us. Every. Single. Day.

Building confidence is essential to effective facilitation, and that includes building confidence not only in yourself but in your learners and in the content. Of the more than 3,500 participants we have worked with across 43 programs in all modalities as ATD facilitators, the most frequent focus area for participants was centered on establishing or maintaining confidence in their performance as trainers. At the end of a rigorous, four-day train-the-trainer program, a participant approached Carrie to thank her for the learning experience and then asked, "How do I get your confidence?" Carrie was surprised by her question, and quickly responded, "You don't. And you shouldn't want to. The real question is, how do you get your confidence?"

Typically, to help trainers establish confidence, we have them identify something they are extremely confident in through an icebreaker activity. It could be something they've mastered with years of practice; it could be something that's a newly acquired skill. Whether it's skiing the wintery slopes in Vermont or baking the most delicate of flourless chocolate cakes or mastering the ubiquitous Excel pivot tables, we all have something we are confident in. During the activity at the start of the train-the-trainer program, participants enter the training reflecting on something they are confident in and sharing with the group the steps they took to build that confidence. Not only does it allow for storytelling and rapport building amongst the group, but it transitions us into the mindset of the program: This learning experience is one of the steps that helps build or maintain your confidence as a facilitator.

Try making a list of the things you're confident in. Like right now. We'll wait.

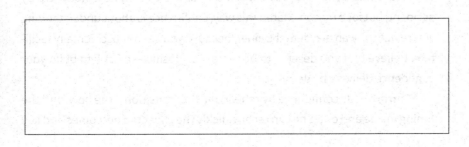

Now, examine how you built that confidence over time and your attitude toward the items on your list. Track how you arrived at success so you can reengineer it into other scenarios. It is through learned experiences, failure, mentoring, practice, skill building, and trial and error that we build our confidence. It is not prescribed by sticking to lists or best practices. When it comes to facilitation—even if you are new to this profession— it will take time to build confidence in yourself, in your learners, and in the content.

With all the certifications and training we complete to ready ourselves for the responsibility and honor of guiding others along their learning journeys, and with all our podcast listening, article reading, and overstuffed trainer toolkits of dos and don'ts, we can get mired in checklists and models and forget how to be ourselves. But what's at risk? Our credibility for one, followed closely by the impact we have.

Mining for stories and examples to bring to the content we are facilitating helps to build confidence in the content. And knowing that the learners have experience can be extremely useful. The learners are yet another facilitation tool. Ask yourself often, "How can I leverage questioning techniques, collaboration, stories, and examples to build the experience and truly serve as a guide to develop talent in others?"

Facilitation in Action

Building Confidence

Jared's confidence aligns to identifying his purpose. Even when he feared trying out facilitation as a potential job, he wanted to give it a try. He was eager to practice improving. He tells himself that as the trainer, he is not there by accident, but for a reason. Stated this way, confidence is about understanding you're not truly an accidental trainer, because you cannot accidentally facilitate. Believe that you deserve to be there. Use positive self-talk to build your confidence delivery by delivery.

Carrie builds confidence by rehearsing the transitions, the flow, and the timing inside and out. She can recall quickly the expected outcomes and key takeaways. She gives herself permission to let go of what may be scripted to allow space for the content to come alive in the moment of learning. She allows what she has absorbed through preparation to come alive the next time she delivers that content to learners. That requires continually letting go of perfection because, in the moments she fails at getting it right (which is often, by the way), she seems to be her most authentic. She embraces the fumbles; she has learned to laugh at herself. It gives learners permission to do the same thing. She's not aiming for perfection or smoothness. She's aiming for connection and impact.

How Do I Translate In-Person Confidence to Being on Camera in the Virtual Classroom?

Do you need to gain confidence in front of the camera for virtual, live online trainings? Setting the atmosphere for a successful virtual training experience depends greatly on your ability to create a positive, comfortable environment that is conducive to learning. If you feel less than confident, your uneasiness can distract learners or render them passive. Here are ways you can trade on-camera awkwardness and uneasiness for confidence and comfort.

Take Pride in What You Project

Present yourself as you would if you were making an impression in person. When behind a camera, it's a bit easier to relax how we present ourselves, how we speak, and how we act. Experts say there's a direct correlation between grooming and clothing and how you think, feel, and behave (St. Louis 2017).

Complete Your Preparation Practice

If you'd normally practice in front of a mirror or record yourself ahead of a face-to-face learning experience, do the same for your virtual courses. The more you practice, the more comfortable you become.

Cap Your Camera Time

For virtual training sessions, it's acceptable to go on camera just for introductions and break announcements as well as to conclude the session. Not only does that reduce your on-camera time, but it also enables learners to better focus on the presented content. Sounds like intentional camera use, right?

Deliver Training From a Distraction-Free Environment

Everything from a cluttered, unprofessional background to unexpected interruptions from pets and loved ones count as distractions. Knowing that you have a clutter-free background and that you're not subject to distractions will help elevate your virtual presence and enable you to devote your total concentration to the course. While you're at it, declutter your desk to enhance your focus on the training.

On-camera confidence can be important whether you're facilitating live online with your camera on for the duration of the course or you're facilitating on camera intermittently during key moments of the learning experience. ATD's live online programs encourage webcams only when it's been intentionally designed into the program to create a positive learning environment or enhance peer-to-peer collaboration. And, to remain aligned to adult learning principles, the learner is invited to turn on their webcam but can choose to remain off camera.

The on-camera confidence of our facilitator team is supported by this policy because they are not being asked to multitask while on camera. They can fully listen and engage with the participants, then turn the webcam back off and continue instruction.

How Do I Balance What My Gut Tells Me to Do and What I've Prepared to Do?

Balance intuition and intention. That means striking a balance between what's natural and honing it for impact with your learners in a moment of need.

It can be helpful to think of how you operate in a typical day. Do you go with your gut in everyday situations, trusting your instincts to guide you? If so, maybe you lean on your intuition more heavily. Alternatively, maybe you start with the why first and leverage your instinct to confirm your gut feeling. Both approaches are powerful and can be leveraged when working to make an impact during facilitation. Our intuition tells us we need to make a change and our intention allows us to choose the best next step that speaks to our facilitation style.

Facilitation is rooted in interpersonal skills. We take the best of these skills, like communication, collaboration, leadership, motivation, active listening, and flexibility, and mesh them together with intention to heighten the impact for our learners.

For example, think of your own experience as a learner. Consider your energy level in an all-day training. How do you feel at the start of the session? Maybe excited, apprehensive, or distracted? One hour before the end of the session in the afternoon, how do you feel? Bored, tired, or clouded with the list of to-dos that awaits you after the training? By inhabiting your own experience as a learner, you can extend empathy to the learners in your training. This approach allows you to balance your intention (the plan you have to conduct a three-part activity in the last hour of the training) with your intuition (which tells you to provide learners a choice in how they experience the content at the end of the day—in a two-part activity or self-directed, informal way to maintain engagement).

Facilitation in Action

Balance Intuition and Intention

Let's say you are piloting new content. For any of us who have done that, it can be a bit daunting. In the moment, we may feel stressed because both intuition and intention are screaming at us.

- **Intuition** tells us, "It won't work" (the content, activities, or delivery).
- **Intention** tells us, "We don't know if the learners will get what they need during this course."

Jared likes to say, "This inner turmoil is what we need to sift through to find the positive impact and intent." This leads to shifts in our delivery. But how do we do this? We feel our intuition saying it won't work—for example, thinking that an electronic discussion board will not work to help learners collaborate in a face-to-face classroom. But if we go with our intuition and say the lesson was designed this way for a reason, the intent may play out. The intent is to allow all learners to be able to contribute in a safe space, which is exactly what the electronic discussion platform is intended to allow.

Strive to find the balance between intuition and intention, always considering your end goal for the learners. Consider what your gut is telling you to do in the moment. What you end up doing in these core moments shines a spotlight on your unique facilitation style.

How Do I Learn to Adapt to Changes as a Trainer?

Would you consider yourself adaptable? Are you able to thrive in the present moment? Can you adjust and flex as needed without getting frazzled? If so, you already have a facilitation skill under your belt! We spoke in chapter 2 about pivoting and also learned that adaptability is central to Darryl's facilitation style. Facilitation is all about adaptability. Modify an activity, flex your facilitator guide to meet the needs of the virtual classroom rather than the face-to-face classroom, adjust your tone to meet the learners' needs, and go with the flow when technology fails. Adaptability helps us pivot when uncertain or complicated moments arise in our training programs. Here are some practical ways to build your adaptability.

Welcome the Challenge

As a facilitator, Darryl relies on instinct to react to the moment. For him, change is viewed as a welcomed challenge. Disruptions can take the learner's mind on a detour from the training. He recalls a training for a new software that was suddenly interrupted by a fire alarm. The fire alarm occurred during one of the key exercises of the class: a simulation activity designed to give learners practice with a new process they will perform back on the job. The fire drill took away valuable learning time at a key juncture of the class. Realizing that the interruption blunted momentum from the activity, upon returning to the classroom Darryl decided not to immediately pick up where they left off in the activity. To get everyone's attention back on the activity, he led the group through a quick recall activity that involved the learners highlighting the steps in the process that were previously covered. He uses short reset activities whenever he encounters interruptions in the classroom.

Plan, Prepare, and Practice

For Nikki, adapting to change that challenges initial intent can be intimidating. This is when she leverages a few reflection questions for support: "What's the big picture here?" (focus more on outcomes, rather than all the details) or "How can we know what could happen unless we try?" (challenge yourself to change). Her typical style relies on structures and routines, but still allows her to try something new for the betterment of the learners. For example, during the COVID-19 pandemic, some course materials were eliminated for safety. Standard classroom materials pre-pandemic included a trainer toolkit of ice-pop sticks for group sorts, wall charts for learner collaboration, and decks of playing cards for team competitions, to name a few. She saw this "no-material classroom" as a challenge. Rather than use the ice-pop sticks as part of the standard icebreaker to form partners, she had learners share their responses via a survey in a mobile polling application. Upon reflection, she realized that the new method worked even better than her previous method. It taught her that trying something new could open positive possibilities, not to mention lighten the load in her trainer toolkit.

Begin building your adaptability by trying one new thing in your next training program. Open your mind to what could occur, and explore new approaches. When something unexpected occurs, practice resilience and quickly recover, flexing your problem-solving skills. The side benefit of adaptability is it's learner focused.

Facilitation in Action

Change the Plan

Nikki once facilitated an all-day virtual training on the topic of instructional design for e-learning. There was prescribed homework that she as the facilitator was supposed to give to the learners at the end of the day that included answering a question by writing a one-page reflection response. She could feel that the energy level in the room was low and that the class was drained. She knew the intention of the lesson plan was to give the assignment. But in the moment, she followed her intuition, pivoted around the plan, and asked the group what they needed.

It sounded like this: "I am sensing that we are drained. I was going to assign some reflection work via a personal writing exercise for homework tonight. I am sensing that the group is spent. What should we do, team? Do we want to make it optional and take a brain break tonight and come back fresh tomorrow?" An important note: The activity Nikki chose to skip was a nice-to-have activity and not essential to meeting a learning objective. Had the activity been directly linked to a learning objective that impacted learners' outcomes at the end of the course, she might have tried a different approach.

All learners agreed to Nikki's modification. She also offered anyone who wanted to do the activity the ability to still submit it for feedback, to allow all learners a choice.

What's Next?

Developing your facilitation style requires time, experience, reflection, and a desire for growth. So, what's next? Start observing facilitation styles in action, *and* start reflecting on your own style using any of the prompts in this chapter. Audit all the training programs you can within and outside your organization. Experience them as a learner. Attend professional development courses and train-the-trainer programs. Engage with colleagues for feedback and normalize constant recalibration of your skills. To help you get started, spend some time with the invitation that follows.

Invitation

Answer the questions below to reflect on your facilitation style. If you're more of a visual person, create a digital mood board using a website like BeFunky.com.

1. When making decisions during facilitation, what do you need to lean into to make those decisions?

   _____

   _____

2. What two facilitation skills are central to your current style?

   _____

   _____

3. What two facilitation skills do you want to hone to grow your facilitation style?

   _____

   _____

4. What are three facilitation skills you are confident in?

   _____

   _____

When your next activity in the classroom does not go as planned, ask yourself, "What do the learners need in this moment?" and then proceed with your intuition. At the conclusion of the training, reflect on the activity to determine the success (or lessons learned) of trying something new.

Chapter 5
Facilitating Across Modalities

Imagine you are cooking your famous chickpea stew for an upcoming dinner with friends. You know the ingredients by heart, the exact temperature and texture that signal the stew has thickened enough for serving. You don't measure the spices anymore because you have perfected the exact amount of a dab and a pinch and the right number of mint leaves to garnish with.

But what happens when you need to cook your famous chickpea stew over a hot plate at a campground? What happens when the pot is so small, the fire is so hot, and the wind is so unforgiving that it takes longer to cook, and you'll have to do several small batches, which affects all your usual estimations? Or imagine you're cooking in your friend's kitchen, where they have a gas stove, not an electric one like you're used to, and despite pulling open every drawer, you can't seem to find the right size of slotted spoon to pull the chickpeas to the top of the stew, and your friend picked up red onions instead of yellow onions and that just won't do for your recipe. What do you do?

You adapt.

You modify your plan.

You take alternative routes, use different tools, and take your existing knowledge and skills and adapt to the environment you're in. As facilitators, we do the same thing when we think of adapting to facilitate in various modalities. We can and should be prepared to translate our skills as trainers and facilitators in any learning modality to support target performance.

For Your Consideration

A Note on Naming Conventions

The different modalities where learning takes place often overlap with different names depending on the industry, organization, team, or even personal preference. Some refer to classroom learning as the *traditional classroom*, the *face-to-face classroom*, or *the in-person classroom*. Some remove *classroom* from their descriptions all together. Similarly, a *blended solution* for one organization may be referred to as *hybrid learning* in another, even though they are notably different. One facilitator may call their live online classroom *vILT* (virtual instructor-led training), while another may refer to it as their *LO* (live online) or *synchronous session*.

For our conversation here, let's use the following definitions adapted from the Talent Development Body of Knowledge (ATD 2019):

▶ **Virtual classroom:** online learning space where learners and the facilitator interact from various locations

▶ **Face-to-face classroom:** also known as traditional learning, the face-to-face classroom brings together the facilitator and learners in person

▶ **Online learning:** technology-enabled training that is asynchronous (self-paced) learning

▶ **Blended learning:** uses several modalities in one curriculum and strategically linking formal, informal, and social learning events

▶ **Hybrid learning:** engages both in-person and virtual learners in the same learning experience with equitable experiences

How Do I Adapt My Facilitation to Deliver in a Different Modality?

The foundational skills of training and facilitation are the same, but how you deploy these skills will take into consideration the modality you are using them in. We know from John Medina's 2008 book, *Brain Rules,* that "the brain doesn't pay attention to boring things." And it's common practice that we should vary our instructional method every six to eight minutes in the face-to-face classroom to maintain engagement and ensure learners are actively doing something, while in the virtual classroom that time shrinks to three to five minutes. The amount of time shifts by modality. The *how* is different.

The reason for developing adaptability in our skill set as trainers has never been more evident than during the COVID-19 pandemic. Within a matter of days, those who were facilitating solely in the face-to-face classroom had to pivot to demonstrate effectiveness in an entirely new modality: the virtual classroom. Some were already facilitating regularly in that space. Some were used to the virtual classroom but were not prepared to be inundated with back-to-back programs in between back-to-back meetings and conversations via Microsoft Teams or Zoom. Nor were we prepared for the frequency with which learners would be using virtual meetings, greatly impacting their approach to the virtual classroom experience.

ATD Education has been offering synchronous, virtual, instructor-led classroom experiences since 2006, and we continually equip our facilitators with tools to help adapt their delivery for the modality they are delivering in. Here are some of the categories that inform our approach in preparing for the virtual classroom, with an example of each:

- **Preparation.** Prepare the materials, yourself, and the environment (including video and audio). Communicate with your virtual producer (if you're lucky enough to have one) ahead of time to ensure you are aligned on program flow and technical needs.
- **Workspace arrangement.** Locate your noise-canceling headset. Fill up a water bottle. Clear your workspace. Hang your timing sheet in front of you. Have your materials within reach.
- **Technology testing.** Arrive to the virtual classroom early to test the features you'll be using, from screen sharing to webcams and breakout rooms. Take yourself on a virtual tour of the space and functionality.
- **Audience engagement.** Smile, even if they can't see you on webcam. Smile, because they can most definitely hear your smile. Inform learners of how you will engage them and ask for

their participation, state the number of breaks they'll get, and most important, embrace the pause. Learners are often simultaneously navigating among materials, thinking, clicking their mouse, and trying to respond in the platform, so their responses or processing time may be delayed.

- **Breakout rooms (and other instructional methods).** Always demo the technical instructions before using the functionality of the platform. Always visit each breakout room to make sure learners have what they need to be successful in the activity.
- **Participant communications (discussion boards, platform announcements, emails, learning management system posts).** So many challenges can be conquered with clear, concise communications. Setting the stage for learning in pre-course communications can be essential to maximizing your time with learners. We strive to send a learner communication two weeks prior to the course, one week prior to the course, throughout the course in a scheduled cadence, and in a post-course follow-up.

Whether delivering training in the face-to-face classroom, virtual classroom, or asynchronous online environment, facilitators guide learners to make a connection between the content and their performance. Each modality provides us the opportunity to impact learning transfer and meet the ever-changing needs of our learners. How we get there may look a little different.

Facilitation in Action

The Lab

The Lab was the first face-to-face classroom Darryl worked in as a facilitator, and it's the place where he experienced many firsts. It was where he toiled in anonymity day after day, session after session, sharpening his skills as a facilitator. He can still feel the crisp air flowing out of the vents above his head at the front of the room. He can still hear the voices of learners buzzing with conversation during activities. He can still remember observing that "aha" moment in learners, when their stance shifts or their eyes widen as if something in their understanding has sparked a physiological reaction.

We're sure you operate today in a place or on a platform where the magic of learning happens like it did in the Lab. Where you make connections with learners across your organization. Where you share knowledge and skills that change their performance. Where you lead activities that produce moments that they return to over the course of their career.

Our classrooms today represent a multitude of flexible and diverse options to support a variety of learning methods and learning preferences. While the training we offer across different modalities will be different, we still can achieve the same learning outcomes.

What Do I Need to Know About Facilitating in the Face-to-Face Classroom Environment?

Over the course of our team's careers, we have been provided numerous opportunities to nurture and counsel new facilitators in the art of successful facilitation in the face-to-face classroom. Facilitating face-to-face offers learners unique opportunities to come together to obtain knowledge, learn new skills, and practice new skills and knowledge in a setting that requires openness and vulnerability.

Successful facilitation in the face-to-face classroom requires facilitators to lean on a broad range of skills to engage all learners in the experience fully. Facilitators are called on to guide the learner's journey all while focusing on group dynamics to help learners work together, make decisions, and identify and solve problems to achieve the learning outcomes. Here's how you can support learning.

Tailor Examples and Analogies

Prepare your practical examples and analogies ahead of time, ensuring they are inclusive and tailored to the learners' context (their organization, their department, their role). Ensure your stories are relevant and relatable for the learners you're working with, and they'll begin offering their stories as well.

Ask and Respond to Questions

Use a variety of questioning techniques to engage all learners. Plan your questions ahead of time and ensure you are rotating question types to yield different responses. Respond to questions by asking for clarity, asking for alternative perspectives from other learners, or by building on what the learner said to tie it back to the outcome. And equally important as planning your questions is not planning them. Allow yourself the flexibility to truly listen to participants' contributions, and ask follow-up questions instinctively in those moments.

Encourage Discussion

It's not about you! (We mean this kindly.) But, it's not about you. Be willing to take a back seat to the discussions that take place. Encourage discussion through storytelling, questioning, and asking for examples from the group to allow peer collaboration and contributions to take center stage.

Lead and Monitor Learners in Activities

Provide instruction and guidance to keep the learning experience progressing through various activities in your programs. Get learners started with clear directions for success, establish alignment with the outcome of the activity, and take time to clarify any confusion before proceeding. Check in with small groups, partners, or the large group during activities to ensure they have what they need to reach the desired outcome. (Hint: Monitoring progress during the activity is the part that typically gets overlooked by trainers.)

Manage Group Dynamics

Learning preferences, behavior styles, motivations—there's a lot to consider as we manage the dynamics of a group of learners. Cognitive science includes the study of the human brain and how it processes information—in short, how we understand understanding. And there are various contextual cues that inform that process. As facilitators, we manage group dynamics by managing conflict in a way that preserves the relationship between the facilitator and the learner, as well as among learners. Additionally, we need the skills to display flexibility and the ability to invite in passive or resistant learners.

Overcome Challenges

First, reframe your approach by *overcoming* challenges to keep the learning experience on track. This requires a display of flexibility, active listening, empathy, and gaining buy-in from the group on how to proceed. We'll go into this a little later in this chapter.

Model Behavior

For some programs, it's essential to model the behavior you're training on (think leadership workshops, effective communication programs, or train-the-trainer sessions). On our team, we believe we are always behavior modeling. In Nikki's software training, she aims to demonstrate flexibility, adaptation, and patience because those are capabilities the learners need to develop as well.

Measure to Ensure That Learning Is Taking Place

Debrief the activity. Ask questions about on-the-job application. Help learners draw meaningful connections from the training to their workflow. Provide ample time for learner questions. Evaluate learner success on meeting learning objectives.

This is by no means an exhaustive list of how we support learning; rather, it's meant to help you begin thinking of what you would add to this list to make it more specific to your own experience. Perhaps bring your team together to explore this list further.

For Your Consideration

Activity: Power of the Exercise

A few years ago, Darryl observed a colleague facilitate a leadership 101 session. The course was mandatory for all newly hired or promoted managers and was viewed as a key part of their development plan. Most participants in the program were being trained to work middle manager roles within their respective divisions. Their primary responsibility was to manage daily operations of their work units. Often, they were tasked with carrying out the overall agenda and vision as communicated to them by their division chief.

During the class, one of the key learning goals was to provide techniques to successfully communicate to direct reports. Darryl's colleague shared an example from an early role in their career, when they were the lead recruiter at the local university. They shared many of the communication challenges they encountered in the role. While the story was relevant, and the concepts were accepted and understood by the participants, the facilitator devised an activity to deepen the learners' understanding of the communication challenges.

In the exercise activity, learners were placed into groups of six, and were asked to sit in pods. The pods were arranged into three rows with one seat at the top in row one, two seats in row two, and three seats in row three. Members of the group could choose their seat before they were given additional guidance. Each pod embarked on a complex communication journey where only written communication was allowed. It was designed to show how the intent of a message is often lost when it is communicated through different levels within an organization.

The learner sitting in the top row was designated as the director. The learners sitting in the second row were designated as department managers. The learners in the third row were designated as unit managers. Each learner was instructed to capture in their words the message that was being communicated to them by their manager. To start the exercise, the facilitator provided a memo for the director to review and quickly summarize in writing. The memo included a fictional new and complex policy that was being implemented by the agency. Using note cards, each row communicated their interpretation of the message that they'd received from the row in front of them. During the debrief, the unit managers in the last row were asked to share their interpretation of the message they'd received. The unit managers each shared different interpretations of the message. The pods quickly discovered that the intent of the message can be lost as it travels through the organization. To wrap up the activity, the class brainstormed approaches to overcome organizational communication challenges.

How Do I Manage Challenges in the Face-to-Face Classroom?

Within our industry, the focus on challenging behaviors is commonly on the person presenting the behavior and how to manage that individual. A quick search of industry blogs and articles will reveal phrases like "managing pesky participants" and "dealing with problem participants." Our ATD facilitator team is focused on achieving learning outcomes and maintaining a learner-centered environment, so we aim to be more interested in *overcoming* the behavior presented and not *managing* the participant exhibiting the behavior. In fact, we teach this approach in our ATD Master Trainer Program. This semantic shift (overcoming versus managing) allows us to depersonalize the behavior when it presents itself and find a way forward to ensure the learning event stays on track. Now, there are moments where you do have to shift into managing a person, but that's not where we aim to begin.

Typically challenges occur in two main categories: challenging situations and challenging behaviors. Whether you're preparing to overcome challenging situations (think technology failure, a power outage, missing materials, illness) or challenging behaviors (think learners responding excessively, distracting other participants, arguing with the validity of the content or credibility of the facilitator), preparation is key. On our team, we subscribe to the value of preparing for what could be and knowing the go-to options in the case of an obstacle. And when all else fails, we strive to remain human and empathetic in our approach.

When facilitating ATD's Training & Facilitation Certificate and the ATD Master Trainer Program, we model and facilitate a few tested techniques that go a long way toward ensuring challenges don't arise and preparing us for when they do.

Leverage Group Commitments at the Start of the Session

If you engage learners in setting the parameters for the learning experience together, rather than telling them how they will participate, they'll be empowered to uphold them. And if they misstep, you're able to reference these commitments to realign the group.

Connect With Your Learners

Before the start of the session, as well as throughout, the work you do to establish moments of connection through conversation, storytelling, one-on-one conversations, or even icebreakers and energizers can cultivate mutual respect. Carrie ensures she finds a way to connect with all learners in some manner before the end of day one for large audiences, and within the first morning of day one for groups of 30 or fewer. Her motto: "I don't just want to connect with them; I want to learn from them in those small moments."

Use Body Proximity and Movement

Moving from one side of the room to the other visually cues a learner that change is occurring, which will in most cases shift their focus from whatever else is happening in the room to what you're doing. Standing near a participant who might be unknowingly presenting a disruptive behavior will usually signal a behavior change as well. It should be said, however, that proximity should be maintained at a respectful distance for everyone's comfort.

Don't Underestimate the Unscheduled Break

Learners don't know your full game plan. They don't know the transition between topics or the expected flow of the program or if your unscheduled break will put you behind time. And they don't know that your unscheduled break at the end of a group discussion, activity, or lecturette is in fact unscheduled. The break serves as a tangible pause, mental and physical, that allows you to reset the energy in the room and proceed thoughtfully once the break is over.

Engage With One-on-One Conversations

The one-on-one conversation is a great way to address a challenging behavior without enabling groupthink. We frame our one-on-one conversations with this process:

1. Check in with the learner.
2. State what occurred clearly and specifically.
3. State the impact the behavior had on the learning and other learners.
4. Pose a question to the learner about how they would like to proceed (holding learners able).
5. Make an ask of the learner moving forward.

Facilitation in Action

How Do We Prepare for What We Don't Know Yet?

In a previous role, Darryl led the new-hire training program at a financial services company. It was the signature training program for his department, and it drew people from across the Mid-Atlantic region of the United States. Over a two-week period, the program demanded a lot from the facilitator to lead the group through extensive guided labs, return demonstrations (or teach-backs), videos, behavior-modeling activities, lectures, simulations, and assessments. In addition, a handwritten file was maintained for each new hire capturing their progress throughout the program.

All of this was done in effort to position the new hires to provide service to customers when they report to their home branch. A typical new-hire cohort would average 10 to 15 new hires every two weeks. This was considered the ideal class size because it matched the number of service machines in the classroom.

Two years into Darryl leading the program, the company announced an acquisition that required the company to nearly triple its workforce. As a result, overnight, the new-hire cohorts swelled from 15 participants to 35 participants. With no co-facilitators in place, no additional workspace, and only a few new service machines added to the class inventory, Darryl had to produce solutions to facilitate the program to meet what was the new normal, with little resources.

He recalls, "I relished this challenge. I was continually asking myself how I could recreate the program and still make it engaging for all the participants. My solution was to create four working stations within the workspace and to create four small groups within the cohort that would work together as they navigated the workstations. The peer collaboration enhanced the learning and the workstations served as mini self-directed activities." The stations were:

- ▶ Workstation 1: Guided Lab and Return Demonstrations
- ▶ Workstation 2: Quiet Space for Reading Assignments
- ▶ Workstation 3: Sales Training Videos
- ▶ Workstation 4: Daily Assessment and Information Search

As we see in Darryl's example, sometimes circumstances force you to adapt and create solutions to meet the needs of your organization and your learners. The end goal of learning transfer remains the same, but the mechanism for reaching that goal might look different.

What Do I Need to Know About Facilitating in the Virtual Classroom?

ATD's 2021 research report *Virtual Classrooms: Leveraging Technology for Impact* found that 98 percent of organizations surveyed used virtual classrooms, and that the leading motivator was safety concerns related to COVID-19 (ATD 2021b). Prior to the pandemic, ATD found that seven out of 10 organizations provided instructor-led virtual training.

Cindy Huggett, an expert in providing interactive virtual training solutions, publishes an annual *State of Virtual Training Report* that provides insights and recommendations for the global talent development community, spanning questions around virtual training duration, participants, webcams, definitions, platforms, challenges, collaboration tools, design time, producers, and the future. The report also contains a category of questions around the "COVID effect," revealing that 91 percent of organizations were offering more virtual training due to

COVID-19, and with the return to offices, 62 percent are or will be offering hybrid classes (Huggett 2021).

Whether you've been facilitating in the virtual environment for years or you've been thrust into the virtual classroom to adapt to current hybrid work trends, we aim to build your appreciation for the space. The ATD virtual classroom brings learners and facilitators together online to move through the experience as a cohort with engagement opportunities, practical application activities, and collaborative discussions.

While the objective of bringing learners together at a specific time to achieve a learning outcome remains the same, the dynamics of leading a virtual class can take some practice. Ask yourself, "How do I engage learners online?" or "How do I know learners are paying attention?" or "How do I hold them able?" Perhaps even, "How do I toggle between my materials and platform without them seeing behind the curtain of my facilitation?" Let's explore.

How Do I Keep Engagement in the Virtual Classroom?

Learners and facilitators alike have various comfort levels training in virtual spaces. There are platforms and chat boxes and webcams to contend with on top of navigating the content and remaining learner focused. However, fostering an environment in which learner participation and engagement flourish rests solely with the facilitator. When facilitators take the right steps to promote and sustain engagement, learners are more attentive and more likely to retain and apply the information shared. Try these strategies in your next virtual classroom to increase engagement.

Open the Flow of Communication

At the start of the session, link pre-course communications to each learner by referencing details from your communications (if acceptable to mention publicly). Build rapport with learners ahead of the first meeting by sending a welcome message one to two weeks before the class. In addition to including tips for using technology and accessing the platform, remind them that the course is for them, and ask them what they need from you. Not everyone will respond, but replying to those who do will have a profound impact. This effort equates to arriving early for the in-person classroom experience to greet learners and get to know them.

Set Virtual Classroom Expectations as a Group

Tee up the session by beginning with, "To maximize and accelerate our learning, we need to agree how we will best work together. Let's add to the whiteboard one thing we need from one another to make this virtual space a productive and positive learning environment. Once you're done, head to the chat to let me know one thing you need from me as well." In this activity, you'll also help learners leverage two of the many feedback and participation tools available in the platform.

Also, consider acknowledging that there will be distractions and provide tips on how to minimize them. For example, give learners permission to close their inboxes and messenger software and power down their phones. Suggest they place a "learning in progress" sign on their door or desk if they have others around them. And, let them know that as they need a break, you encourage them to take it when they need it and come back to the learning space when they are able. Providing that choice builds rapport.

Hold Learners Accountable

(Or, if you read chapter 1, able.) You could start off by saying, "We're going to be asking you to engage with the content and each other often throughout our program. We have a variety of tools at our disposal to do so, with the chat feature, our interactive whiteboards, webcams, and your audio. We'll be using all these methods in our program. If there's something I can do to help you make the most of our virtual classroom, please feel free to private message me."

Explain that everyone is required to engage in the discussion and activities. Agree on a signal that learners can use to inform others that they are away from the computer or need a break, such as a coffee cup emoji or turning off their webcam to signal they've stepped away. Also, let them know that producers (if you have one) are monitoring participants and will note when learners are gone too long.

Keep Learners Active

This can be as simple as saying, "Xaivian, I'm coming to you for the next question" or "Everyone, type one word in the chat that describes how you're feeling." Those simple nudges help keep learners alert and active during the virtual class. As facilitators, we should constantly examine what we can do to maintain engagement above and beyond the designs we are working with. Do we need to upskill on the virtual platform we are using? Do we need to take more virtual classroom courses to experience them as a learner? Do we need to audit a variety of facilitators and their approaches? Do we need to approach the tools we use for engagement as a method for furthering learning outcomes? On our team, it's yes to all these questions. When your ideas for virtual training engagement start to run dry, we suggest Kassy LaBorie's *Interact and Engage! 75+ Activities for Virtual Training, Meetings, and Webinars* (2022) to jumpstart your ideas. Here's how you can support learning:

- **Use platform tools to enable learning.** Regardless of which learning platform you use (Adobe, WebEx, Teams, Zoom), become deeply familiar with the tools at your disposal to engage learners. Leverage a variety of tools and provide choice to your learners to respond how they are most comfortable (chat, audio, whiteboard).
- **Guide learners.** Dial up your task-based dimension of training delivery. As you guide learners through a virtual classroom, they not only need guidance with where the content and discussion is taking them; they also need to know which tool to use and when.
- **Demonstrate proficiency in using the technology.** Don't fear the technology. Don't tiptoe around it. Dive in and learn everything you can, and audit other facilitators leveraging the technology

and tools available to expand your familiarity, including the accessibility features available on a specific platform.

- **Set virtual expectations for learner participation.** It's essential to guide learners on how they can learn online, with either a quick tutorial, tour, or even a few tips for engagement. ATD Education virtual classroom sessions all begin with a tour of the platform tools so we can prepare learners for how to not only learn in the virtual classroom but navigate the program.

How Do I Manage Challenges in the Virtual Classroom?

Some virtual sessions can run without any challenges or disruptions, but as facilitators we should plan for them to happen each time we log on to our virtual sessions. You may experience back-to-back disruptions that range from blaring building fire alarms to mass technical glitches that can cause a group to go offline. Such interruptions can throw off a class's energy—not to mention the schedule. How do you as the facilitator recover?

Disruptions are just that—disruptive. But here is how you can get yourself and your learners aligned to keep the learning experience on track.

Acknowledge the Disruption

Regardless of whether the disruption occurred on your or the learners' end or whether it was technical in nature, call it out to recapture their attention. For example, ask participants to raise their hand or put a green check in the chat if they have experienced similar situations in the past. You may even use a little humor in acknowledging the disruption if that suits your facilitation style. Your goal, however, is to identify it and move on.

Ease Anxiety

Disruptions on the learners' side can be distressing for them. In such situations, ease their anxiety by reassuring them that everything will be OK.

Let them know that there are options available for them to get back up to speed once they are resettled. Options can include buddying up with someone after class or viewing the recording later to review parts they may have missed.

Always Have Multiple Backup Plans

When something unexpected happens, you may need to pivot—quickly. Think through pivot strategies ahead of time. When prepping the material, note slides you can move past or combine with a previous or later discussion, and identify the activities learners can complete later on their own rather than during the session. In determining which content to retain or omit, ask yourself what will have the most impact on reaching your desired end goal. The key to a successful pivot is to let your original learning objectives be your guide.

Involve Learners in Your Go-Forward Plan

At the end of the day, your course is designed for the learners. One strategy to recover from a major disruption is to poll the class—for example, ask learners whether they can move forward with the program or if they need a break after a disruption. Doing so enables you to gauge where they are mentally and energetically while honoring their need to reset. Likewise, it is a way to involve them as co-collaborators of their learning experience.

How Do I Move My Face-to-Face Classroom to Virtual Classroom Training Quickly?

Ah, the tricky adverb at the end of that question changes everything: *quickly*.

Our heads can spin as we try to brainstorm how the magical, engaging eight-hour face-to-face experience we are used to facilitating could possibly fit into a shortened e-learning module or multi-session virtual classroom experience while still maintaining effectiveness and engagement. The first thing we need to realize and accept is that the training will be different. We should not expect it to be the same experience. But can we achieve the same learning outcomes through a different modality?

Absolutely. The key is to ensure that we are successfully setting up our learners to meet the learning objectives. We must focus on the structure and purposefully organize the course for the new environment.

Global pandemic or not, we need to be ready to act on short notice to modify our training materials to accommodate shifting environments. Maybe you have company travel bans, a global workforce, or a lack of facilitator resources. In our experience, we have seen all of these, so being able to train employees virtually or asynchronously is an invaluable must-have capability.

To get your content online quickly and effectively, let's explore a few ideas to jump-start the process.

Make Sure Your Content Is Valid and Relatable

Before you think about adapting any of your current material from the face-to-face classroom to virtual training, check to see if the content is outdated. If it is, get rid of it! Sometimes we are creatures of habit and provide training to provide training because it is what we have always done.

What good does it do to exhaust yourself on a topic or angle that no one cares about or puts into practice? For example, has the organizational culture changed so that the content, as currently presented, is irrelevant? Similarly, does the training relate to "how things are really done around here"? If not, it doesn't make sense to repurpose it.

Further, this might mean making sure your e-learning training is current with the last update of the program—that is, that the version of the software hasn't changed since you've developed the course. For example, has a software update changed the look and feel of an application since the course was developed? If so, be sure to revise any screenshots accordingly. Regarding organizational systems, are processes still handled the way the job aid outlines? Now is the time to make sure your content will help learners be effective and productive.

Make Each Project Development Step Mini

Even though you're being asked to quickly move your face-to-face training into a virtual modality, it still has to meet learning objectives. When you're crunched for time, instead of skipping a step altogether, do a mini needs assessment. Rather than not asking any questions when starting a learning project, ask one or two, such as, "What does success look like once learners complete the training?" Then list key skills, behaviors, and tasks that learners must do differently after the training.

Another mini step in an onboarding example is to ask the new employee's manager, "What can we do to improve the new employee's experience and ability to be productive?" Or check with two employees who have been in the department for one to two years, asking, "What one thing would have made it easier to get up to full productivity had you known it in your first month?"

Only Include the Essentials

Leave out all the nice-to-haves. This will immensely trim down the content.

Include Tasks for Learners to Complete

An effective learning program requires more than a set of clickable PowerPoint slides. The learner needs to experience real-life scenarios, try out tasks, and receive feedback along the way. An extrinsic reward like a smiley face and a thumbs-up icon at the end isn't enough.

An example of this in a virtual classroom would be a knowledge check question, when a facilitator asks learners to respond with a green check or red X, then calls on a learner to hear more and gives personalized feedback. Or, when a facilitator takes a poll of the audience and responds based on the results. Or, when there is a breakout activity, and the facilitator debriefs based on the results that learners came up with in their assigned small groups. It's still all about trying it out and letting the learners practice.

For an onboarding program done via asynchronous online training, you may assign new employees the task of logging on to the intranet to find answers to a series of questions, such as, "In the IT department, how many direct reports does manager Alex have?" and "Which HR staffer handles employee benefit questions, such as healthcare flexible spending?"

Avoid Importing PowerPoint Slides From an ILT Course

In ATD's E-Learning Instructional Design Certificate and ATD's Articulate Storyline programs, Nikki suggests avoiding importing PowerPoint slides from the face-to-face training course. Why? Because face-to-face training and e-learning are different learning modalities. The content may be the same, but the experience does not translate the same way when placed into the online space.

For example, what happens in e-learning when animations are supposed to occur? Or when the facilitator should click to build slides? Or when there is supposed to be a participant discussion occurring? These are all reasons to redesign when changing modality.

Find a Tool That Makes It Easy for You to Build the Program

There is an abundance of e-learning tools, and it can be daunting to know where to start. Nikki prefers Articulate 360 Storyline and RISE but also recommends that designers do their research to weigh the pros and cons of varying tools.

Remember, it may seem like a lot of work up front, but there are immense benefits once your content is online. E-learning has benefits for the learner and the organization. The learner receives a personalized experience and can complete the self-directed learning in their own time. For the organization, the learning is easy to track; the content being delivered is consistent; and there are decreased expenditures due to reduced travel, lower facilitator costs, and decreased time spent at the training event.

What Do I Need to Know About Facilitating in the Asynchronous Online Environment?

When viewing your favorite series on television, you have a multitude of options available today, more so than a few decades or even a few years ago. Whether at home or on the road, on the television or on our mobile phone, streaming technology allows for the opportunity to see our favorite shows on demand, at a time that is convenient for us. The same technology that entertains us is available to support us in our work environment.

The ATD *2021 State of the Industry* report revealed that at the average organization, self-paced online delivery (e-learning) accounted for 32 percent of training hours, an increase from 26 percent the year before (ATD 2021a). Asynchronous e-learning can be accessed using laptops, computers, smartphones, and tablets at a time convenient for the learner.

Technology makes learning readily available to fit the lifestyle and needs of the modern learner. The asynchronous environment allows learners to access course content when it is most convenient for them, allowing them to learn at their own pace. So where do facilitators fit into the asynchronous modality? Do they belong there at all?

At ATD, we facilitate the asynchronous course experience with an aim to serve as a learning guide, recognizing that learners are seeking to tap into our knowledge and expertise for topics for which they need additional context and practical examples. We aim to demonstrate organization, pay attention to detail, create cultural norms, encourage participation, enhance and connect collaboration points, and monitor group dynamics. We get opportunities to fill in the blanks and respond to learners' questions as they navigate the course, all while encouraging learners to interact with one another using the design elements provided by the course design, like discussions, projects, and polls. The key to asynchronous facilitation is to provide this guidance as needed, remembering that your presence should not be a barrier to learner progress.

Communication is essential in the asynchronous environment. When learners ask a question or complete an assignment, they are seeking meaningful feedback and they want to receive it as soon as possible. For instance, set clear expectations for when you will respond to learners and the degree of detail for each response and aim to include at least one practical example in that response. Asynchronous facilitators can also connect learners to information, tools, and resources that are pertinent to the topic. While this additional content is not required, it is a good added touch to deepen learners' understanding of the topic.

Here's how you can support learning:

- **Guide the learning experience.** Connect learners to information and one another.
- **Serve as first point of contact.** Demonstrate organization, quick response times, and the ability to read between the lines in learner comments, posts, and questions. Set your ideal response time and communicate it to learners.
- **Set learner expectations for participation.** Model the level of interaction and quality of discussions in your interactions with learners and in setting expectations with the group.
- **Track learner progress.** Aim to encourage participation that is constructive, positive, active, and inclusive. Remove barriers that inhibit learning and progress.
- **Encourage discussion among peers and between the learner and facilitator.** Synthesize information, discussion threads, and resources. When replying to one question or comment, connect that learner to another learner's post that may illuminate a new perspective or similar perspective.

How Do I Leverage Video in Asynchronous Facilitation?

A three-to-five-minute video facilitation distributed asynchronously to the learners in your online learning cohort can go a long way toward creating a positive learning environment, humanizing the digital experience, and reminding learners that you are in fact there to support and guide their experience if they need you. But when facilitating on video, you can often rerecord yourself into oblivion as you aim to be clear, concise, and, honestly, try not to scratch an itch or make a silly face on camera. Here are some tips to make your next recording a breeze.

Be Prepared; Don't Wing It

For some video shoots you may have a teleprompter, but for others you may not have one. Be sure to review and practice your talking points before the video shoot. Practice will position you to sound authentic to the learner. If you are making it up as you go, your learners will see it and the video's distractions could have an adverse impact on the learning goal.

Imagine Whom You Are Speaking To

Facilitating on video can feel jarring because it is much different from what we are accustomed to in the classroom. We are used to getting our cues from our learners. A way to overcome this is to imagine the learner you are speaking to. Producers give us direction on where to look in each camera shot, so as you look directly into the camera, speak to the learner you have in your mind.

Embrace Mistakes

Even the best talent on camera forgets a point, flubs a word, and makes mistakes. It's OK; we are all human and we make mistakes. Whether you are working with a producer or producing your own video, shoot multiple takes for each topic. This will give you plenty of content to edit together the best possible product.

What Do I Need to Know About Facilitating a Blended Learning Program?

Blended learning uses a variety of components strategically linked across a variety of modalities. In Carrie's experience designing and delivering blended learning solutions, the "strategically linked" part of that statement is imperative. Without intentionally linking content across modalities, you end up with a buffet of disparate parts that make sense on their own but not necessarily together. As a facilitator and designer of blended programs, Carrie wants to find ways to link an asynchronous module to an activity the facilitator will conduct in the face-to-face classroom, so the learners begin making connections between the content areas.

A great example of a blended program is ATD's Master Trainer Program, which is a blend of asynchronous self-paced learning and a live online or in-person classroom experience, where the components of each modality link to the discussions, activities, and content to achieve learner outcomes. What learners achieve during weeks one through three asynchronously in the eight-week program prepares them for what they will be doing during week four, when they come together in the face-to-face or virtual classroom to practice their skills.

In the blended learning environment, learners can share information with one another and collaborate in group exercises and activities while still engaging with their facilitator before, during, and after the program. A blended learning program strategically links various media into one learning program, combining informal and formal learning approaches. The blended learning format enables learners to learn at their own pace during specific intervals of the program and provides more opportunities to gain a deeper understanding of course content.

So, what is the role of the facilitator in a blended learning program? With the many moving parts of a blended course, the facilitator is the link, encouraging learners to take full advantage of all that a blended course offers. Not only do we provide instruction as we would in the classroom, but we also set expectations for learners on how to engage and collaborate with one another online. Most important in a blended program is to help link the various experiences in each modality to one another. For instance, if they are reading an article and doing research on an assigned topic, ensure that when you are together in the in-person portion of the blend you are incorporating that pre-work in an activity or teach-back.

Blended programs really are the best of all worlds. To support a blended learning program, combine the suggestions from this chapter's section on asynchronous facilitation, face-to-face facilitation, and virtual facilitation. Your focus is to build cohesion around the components of the program, measure the learning, and guide the blended experience.

As we learned at the start of the chapter, we define *hybrid learning* as a mixture of in-person learning and online audiences. The goal of hybrid learning is to ensure that all learners have an equitable auditory and visual learning experience to achieve outcomes.

Facilitation in Action

An On-the-Job Blend

When Nikki worked as a new hire trainer for a software development company, she worked alongside cohorts of learners onboarding for three-month blocks of time. For those three months, Nikki facilitated training sessions on various topics with the cohort, enabling them to collaborate with one another when they came together to learn in person and during asynchronous learning moments as well.

What made this program different was that the organization prioritized on-the-job training as a part of the formal learning event using two programs: Ask Me Anything and Department Field Trips.

Ask Me Anything was a once-a-week event that was an optional, informal open forum for face-to-face or virtual connection. The idea was to create a safe space for new hires to voice their challenges on process and to work through them together as a team. Many new hires had similar situations and benefited from hearing solutions. They would take actual work examples and brainstorm how to work through them in the best way possible. The low-pressure environment allowed for free-flowing conversations and provided learners with validation and support.

Department Field Trips involved the new hires spending one-hour blocks of time visiting team members from another department. For example, a software project manager would visit the customer care department, the marketing team, the sales staff, and so on. During that time, the new employee would observe the tasks, roles, and situations that came up in the natural flow of work. Even though it was not the role the learner was going to have on the job, it gave them the inside scoop as to what that department did and how it fit into the larger organizational puzzle. Of course, the field trips also helped to build relationships, which are a cornerstone to success as a new hire.

Facilitation in Action

The Blended Recreation Programming Series

Darryl served as the training manager for a parks and recreation agency for a municipality in the suburbs of Washington, DC. In one of his first tasks, he conducted a training needs assessment. The assessment uncovered a significant gap in knowledge and know-how between seasoned personnel (20 or more years of industry experience) and personnel new to the industry (fewer than 10 years of industry experience) in programming for parks and recreation facilities.

To address the gap, he partnered with the local community college to develop a learning solution designed to provide new professionals with background on programming for recreation facilities. The initial offering of the program drew 25 professionals from divisions across the county by offering seven workshops on program scheduling, special event planning, community engagement, and more. The program was facilitated by seasoned professionals with a deep educational background in recreation, parks, and leisure. For the first three years, the program was offered entirely in person at facilities throughout the county.

The experience quickly became a signature program as members of each cohort connected well with the facilitator and gained the foundational knowledge to successfully plan for their park or recreation facility. Many of the participants gained more responsibilities for programming within the agency and earned promotions because of their participation in the program.

As the program evolved, so did the resources Darryl had in the training department. In the summer, prior to year four of the program, he was able to procure the agency's very first learning management system (LMS). The LMS was packaged with an extensive e-learning offering of management courses.

For years, participants from each cohort indicated that the required attendance for the seven workshops was the biggest challenge. While they enjoyed the program, it was often challenging for them to get coverage for their absence at their facility. It got to the point where some potential learners rejected invitations to participate in the program.

With the new LMS in place, and recognizing the availability concern expressed by participants, the program switched to a blended approach for year four. The in-person workshops were cut from seven to three, and e-learning content was created for access on the LMS. Content covering leadership and management concepts was taken from the in-person workshop and converted into e-learning courses and project assignments.

The change to the blended format generated new excitement for the program. The year four cohort appreciated the scheduling of fewer in-person workshops while enjoying the ability to complete the online assignments at their convenience. The added benefit of the LMS allowed participants to communicate with one another and collaborate on their project assignments.

The program was adopted in 2019 by the Maryland Recreation and Parks Association, and still runs today.

What's Next?

ATD's *2021 State of the Industry* report looked at how organizations distribute learning content to employees. In-person, instructor-led classroom training declined from 41 percent of hours allotted to training to 18 percent. While this number is no doubt impacted by widespread health concerns, it reveals a transition to digital learning that has opened our eyes to a new normal (ATD 2021a).

Invitation

To prepare for what's next in how learning can take place and where, make a list of possible delivery modalities (mobile; augmented, virtual, and mixed reality [AR, VR, MR]; asynchronous; virtual) that can be used for delivering workplace learning.

_____

_____

Now, circle the two items that you feel the most resistance toward. Next, dive in to learning about those things you are most resistant to first. Take a course that primarily uses that specific modality to experience the content delivered that way as a learner would, read case studies of how organizations have implemented these tools, and engage colleagues in exploratory conversations about how your programs could be enhanced by a specific delivery medium.

In short, we subscribe to this notion and often tell our learners: Go where you're most reluctant to go first.

Chapter 6
Facilitating for Impact

We all know the importance of measuring the impact of training. But besides a few questions on a survey or a smile sheet to determine how learners feel about a program, how are we really measuring our impact as facilitators? How do we identify moments of impact when they occur and, perhaps more important, how do we create more of them?

The impact we have on an individual as well as a group of learners involves a little awareness and change rolled together into one: the awareness of seeing an idea or a concept in a different way, and the willingness or motivation to change their behavior based on that awareness. This is the core of what we as facilitators hope to accomplish. We strive to influence each learner we encounter. In fact, that is our responsibility.

At first glance, *impact* sounds very nebulous, especially when using words like *awareness* and *motivation*. How do we impact learners when the word itself feels so intangible? Isn't that too grandiose of an ambition?

In this chapter, we'll tackle adopting a learner-focused approach, how to pivot and adjust in the moment to learner needs, and how you can use questioning and listening techniques to support the impact your facilitation has on workplace performance.

How Do I Ensure My Facilitation Is Learner Focused?

Carl Rogers's learner-centered approach stems from the belief that "we cannot teach another person directly; we can only facilitate [their] learning," and this approach has clear implications for facilitators. In short, we toss out our expectations and what we may want, and instead focus on supporting what the learners need and want to be successful. This may mean that the heavily orchestrated and rehearsed story that you have planned to drive home a key point of your training may have to wait in lieu of making way for a learner's example or story. Maybe in the moment of facilitation, the learners are grasping the concept and sharing their own stories. That's when we tell ourselves, "It's not about me; it's about the learners." That mantra has saved us many times from overriding what the learners need in favor of what we want as the facilitators.

Facilitation in Action

Moving From Task-Oriented to People-Oriented

Nikki was facilitating a train-the-trainer program for a full cohort of enthusiastic attendees who were all apprehensive about their demonstration of skills, a key component to course completion. One student was very new to the world of facilitation, and she compared herself against the others as she moved throughout the program. Nikki's goal for her and all the attendees was to ensure that they had the tools they needed to be successful for the skills demonstration and to be high performers when they got back on the job.

Nikki's past self would have remained task-oriented, thinking, "OK, I need to stick to the timing guide, deliver the content, and ask questions." Instead, she recognized that a different set of facilitation skills would need to be leveraged to the level of experience her group had. She began practicing active listening, sharing her stories and examples from the beginning of her own career to provide relatable examples and model authenticity. As she transitioned to this people-oriented approach, she asked herself,

"What do the learners need?" and "How can I facilitate them to encourage and challenge each other to make the best possible outcome?" Nikki let go of her own agenda to meet learners where they were.

When it came time for the learners' skills demonstration, Nikki watched each one of those attendees shine.

Pure joy flooded over her when her least-experienced attendee effortlessly showcased almost every skill that they had discussed. Nikki and everyone else saw growth in her performance. Nikki thought, "Wow! Look at that!" She now truly knows what it means to deliver a learner-centered approach.

Did you notice the subtle yet important shift in Nikki's approach? It wasn't that she completely abandoned her materials and timing, but they were not the sole driver of her facilitation approach. The needs of her learners focused her attention and influenced the choices she made so she could support their exploration and meet them where they were.

Learner-centered theory originated with Carl Rogers, a psychologist credited with developing the person-centered approach in therapy. The core principle of person-centered therapy is that each person has what they need to find the answers they are looking for, but sometimes they need help navigating their inner selves. It was from this approach that Rogers expanded the concept into education, developing five hypotheses for learner-centered education. You can find the original hypotheses in Table 6-1 (Rogers 1951), accompanied by our interpretation for facilitation and suggested tactics to use to apply the concepts in practice.

Every decision we make comes back to what the learner needs in the moment to be successful. Adopting a learner-centered approach involves the learner in the experience to a high degree and may offer an opportunity to stretch our skill set to align to what the learner needs. If we are focused on making an impact on learners, we are most likely making an impact on ourselves, trying new things, or delivering concepts in new ways.

Table 6-1. Person-Centered Learning Theory

Original Hypothesis	Meaning in Facilitation	Tactics
A person cannot teach another person directly; a person can only facilitate another's learning.	We are all a compilation of our experiences; therefore, what the student experiences is more important than what the teacher does. Each student will learn through the lens of their past experiences.	Actively ask and assess what learners need in the moment to be successful. Make learning interactive; give opportunities for learners to experience the content.
A person learns significantly only those things that are perceived as being involved in the maintenance or enhancement of the structure of self.	Learners focus on what is relevant to themselves, their priorities, and what motivates them.	Involve learners and their stories by linking them to the content. Ensure learners generate their what's in it for me (WIIFM) for the experience.
An experience that involves a change in the organization of self tends to be resisted through denial or distortion of symbolism.	We do not like to be wrong, especially concerning deeply held beliefs. We may actively resist new or different ideas that threaten our identity or self-esteem.	Create a space where all perspectives are valued. Set parameters at the start of the session for interactions and create a space where questioning of ideas is encouraged.
The structure and organization of self appears to become more rigid under threats and to relax its boundaries when completely free from threat.	The perception of mental and emotional safety within the classroom is one of the biggest influences for learners to share and engage with in the process of learning.	Encourage learning and growth, changing beliefs and behaviors when presented with new information. Build rapport with learners; create an environment of healthy discussion and debate.
The educational situation that most effectively promotes significant learning is one in which threat to the self of the learner is reduced to a minimum and differentiated perception of the field is facilitated.	Framing learning as a collaborative experience removes the directive power struggle from the traditional relationship of teacher to student. Facilitators are not omnipotent; they are also adult learners and should acknowledge their limits.	Model a learning mindset; be open to learning from and with your learners. Share your own experiences with the content, especially any struggles you overcame or questions you worked through.

Facilitation in Action

Taking Risks for Yourself and Your Learners

Darryl taught a new hire training program for bank tellers in which they watched the same lecturettes, videos, and scenarios that had been part of the program for years. It was a vital program to set employees up for success at the beginning of their employment. The business needed this training to take place, so he watched and listened to learners, knowing they would tell him what risks and new things they could try together. Whenever he had a group that filled the room with chatter and energy, he'd look for opportunities for collaboration. At times, the training called for independent reflection. He sometimes changed the activity to allow for peer collaboration and simulation instead to invigorate the content.

When Darryl started making these small but important changes, it was reflected positively in the feedback. The participants felt more confident when they dispersed to their branches after the training, as they applied their new skills on the job. It was a risk, of course, to change activities and his approach, but the intent behind the risk was to have a greater impact on their course experience and what would transfer to job performance improvement.

We must have a willingness to take risks to expect bigger rewards, both for ourselves and for our learners.

We have all been in the back of the room watching a facilitator make decisions based on the content or their own comfort. It isn't necessarily the wrong decision, but it is shying away from risk and reward. In Darryl's example, notice he didn't change the goal of the activity. He changed how he executed the activity to engage the learners, meeting them where they were, and putting their experience above the predetermined plan. These small but impactful changes are what we call pivoting, and it is a crucial ability on the path to mastering facilitation.

What Does It Mean to Pivot? And How Do We Know When to Do It?

Pivoting is just as it sounds: a small change in direction, or a necessary adjustment needed throughout the course experience. Even if you've done all the necessary preparations for the program, there are a variety of situations that may require you to change your approach.

Some of the most common that we encounter are when the participants of our training program may know more or less than we expected. Perhaps our instructional method for an activity isn't working as well as we anticipated. Or we recognize due to an influx of learner questions that we need to spend more time on a particular section. We can't always predict when we will need to pivot, but we've listed common situations that often require us to adjust our original plan in some way in Table 6-2. What would you add?

Table 6-2. Common Pivot Moments

Situation	Examples
Changes in head count	Participants do not attend, or leave during the training
Technology issues or errors	Slides or videos not loading, polling software lagging, projectors or screens not working, learning platform errors
WIIFM (what's in it for me)	Learner goals may not align to program objectives or organizational outcomes
Materials issues	Insufficient number of supplies, or materials are missing altogether; you have an outdated version of the materials that doesn't align to participant materials; participants didn't bring a device required for participation
Content challenges	Confusion of concepts, instructions, or activities; participants challenge the validity of the content
Hot button topics	Current events within the world, local culture, or organizational context that must be addressed
Timing	Activities taking longer than expected, needing to make up the time somewhere else in the program
Challenging situations or behaviors	Passive learners, inappropriate comments, nonparticipatory behaviors

To prepare for these moments, our ATD facilitator team finds it helpful to list all the scenarios that could require a pivot in the moment of facilitation (in addition to the list we started earlier). Then, we aim to work through the following questions:

- If I stick with the original plan, what is the possible outcome?
- If I change the plan, what are the consequences of that change?
- What is the preferred way forward that is best for the learners and the course outcomes?

You might be thinking, "When do I do this?" You work through the list and questions at two times: during your preparation process and in the moment. (Hint: The preparation part greatly affects your ability to adjust on the fly.) Let's look at some examples of this.

- **Pivoting is what we do for every class.** There is no perfect environment, no matter how well we prepare. Whenever Darryl works with a client, especially on multiday programs, he always involves the stakeholders to informally assess their impressions on day one to guide the following days. It means being proactive from the outset to continually discover opportunities along the course of the delivery and preparing to pivot based on that feedback.
- **We are the GPS, and our learners are the drivers.** For Jared, the learners determine the destination (their goals for the training), and we plan a route to get them there. They might take an unexpected turn, and we need to find a way to off-road or detour most effectively (and safely). We plan based on potential delays, construction, and traffic patterns, but at the end of the day the driver can choose where they want to go, and it is our responsibility to guide them.
- **We must ask for feedback to know how to pivot.** Nikki always checks in with learners throughout a program to ask what is working for them. The ideas they have for changes inform if— and potentially how—she needs to adjust.

- **We find ways to orchestrate pivoting in the moment to gain practice with adapting in the moment.** When Carrie observes that an instructional method isn't resonating with a particular group of learners, she'll challenge herself to try a different instructional method later in the program and measure if that change had greater resonance. If a participant asks a question that provides her the opportunity to reinforce former discussions or activities, she'll adjust the agenda or where she's going to go next in the content based on that question. She also tells the learners in her train-the-trainer programs that the participants don't know what your plan is. So the only way they know you changed the plan is if you tell them. Choose to adapt, commit to the change, and continue evaluating the effectiveness of your approach.

Pivoting is not an exact science. Sometimes a situation makes it very clear when we need to adjust, like when we only have 30 minutes left in a session and at least 90 minutes of content to get through. In this case, we need to make choices about what we can and cannot cover in our remaining time.

At the risk of sounding too vague, you will know the moment when you encounter it. We can often feel when an experience is veering off a productive path. We can see the confused looks, blank stares, guarded body language, questions about content we just explored—or, worse, no questions at all. Perhaps we are even facing active resistance or pushback, which can often be the case with misaligned or misunderstood WIIFMs and content challenges. In our experience, the easier part is noticing when we need to pivot. The more challenging part is knowing how to pivot.

How Do I Adjust in the Moment to Learner Needs?

There is no single right way to adapt to learner needs. This is a skill that develops over time with experience, creativity, luck, and being well-prepared with one or several back-up plans. Mostly, it involves trying new things. The more scenarios we encounter where we need to pivot, the more accustomed we are to pivoting. We will also have more ideas and options in our back pocket with our accumulated experience.

To pivot, we start with recognizing the need—acknowledging what isn't working or what is a barrier to our learners' success. After that, it is really open as to what change we make. Ask yourself: "What do I need learners to get out of this experience? What changes can I make to honor the original intention?" Some activities are low stakes in terms of how we move learners through them; others may be central to the learning objectives and are required to be run in a specific way. It doesn't mean we can't pivot, but we must figure out a way to do it successfully.

For example, imagine you are running a training program with 30 people in a small room. You planned to run a relay race exercise with wall charts posted around the room that learners would move between. Because it is a race, they may move rather quickly. With so many learners and limited space, you feel it is too crowded to run the exercise safely and effectively. So, you share your original plan and intention with your learners and ask them: "Based on what we had hoped to do, how would you like to proceed?" You facilitate a brief brainstorm and discussion, landing on the idea of having learners stay seated and passing a paper and pen among the teams instead.

Here, we still retain the competitive spirit of the exercise and leverage teams, but we adapt how the exercise occurs for learner safety and comfort within the space. We also create the opportunity to gain credibility with our learners and involve them in the process of learning. We acknowledge with our learners that our original plan may not work and ask for their ideas in moving forward successfully together.

A high degree of questioning and listening skills is crucial to involve learners in the process of pivoting. These skills are also priceless in our pursuit of impact.

How Do Questioning and Listening Support Impact?

Questioning techniques and listening skills dance together, like yin and yang, balancing each other out as they flow through a conversation or learning experience.

Questioning provides opportunities for learners to think, reflect, explore, and share.

Listening provides opportunities for learners to hear, absorb, digest, and analyze.

When facilitating, we focus on how we ask the questions as well as how we respond to the questions in equal parts. It's how we guide and challenge learners and check for understanding to measure progress or learning.

In our programs, we guide facilitators to strive for open-ended questions with a clear purpose that are clearly stated. When posing questions, you should use a variety of approaches to increase engagement:

- **Overhead:** Pose to the large group.
- **Directed:** Pose to an individual or a group of individuals.
- **Round Robin:** Pose to the large group (and invite everyone to answer).
- **Redirect:** Redirect a learner's question to you back to the group.

One model that resonates with learners of ATD's Master Trainer Program is the FOID model of questioning by facilitator Donna Steffey, president of Vital Signs Consulting. The model provides a structure for not only preparing questioning techniques but evaluating the variety of questions used. Let's take a look at the model:

- **Fact:** Questions focused on who, what, when, and where
- **Opinion:** Questions aimed at gathering learner insights, perspectives, and opinions
- **Importance:** Questions that ask about significance or the why
- **Do:** Questions focused on what learners will do as a next step

The ATD facilitator team uses this model not only to ensure that we've planned a variety of questions that satisfy these four categories, but to assess where we tend to lean more naturally. For instance, Jared relies heavily on the importance questions and Carrie relies heavily on the opinion questions. Knowing that, each can strategically prepare questions that pull from the other categories to create balance.

As we pose questions to our learners, we also need to listen to their responses. As we listen, we tune in to the learner's words and stop our minds from moving forward while still engaging in the current discussion. Active listening to learner responses helps draw links between a learner's contribution and the content or previous comments. Additionally, listening for responses creates an opportunity to deepen the learning by building on what participants say.

Practice building on learner comments through any of the following methods:

- **Paraphrasing** (used to confirm understanding and maintain engagement)
  - What I heard you say was . . . Is that correct?"
  - "I'm connecting to what you said about . . . ?"
- **Follow-up questions** (used to remain learner-centered and create collaboration)
  - "Who has something to add to Raheem's answer?"
  - "Tell me more about that?"
  - "What if [fill in the blank]?"
  - "What topic does that relate to that we've covered in the course so far?" (linking comment to content)
  - "How will this affect you back on the job?"

We can leverage these skills for the benefit of our learners, but if we model them correctly and create a safe, open environment, we can encourage our learners to use these skills for themselves during the learning experience. When learners use these skills and begin leaning on one another, asking questions of their peers, we know we are in the process of having an impact on learners.

Our go-to questions to increase impact with learners are presented in Table 6-3. What would you add to this list? Once you've completed the list, aim to use one or two new questions in your next training delivery.

Table 6-3. Questions for Impact

Question	Purpose
What could this look like in your role or organization?	• Encourage job transfer • Provide relevance • Establish readiness to learn
What would you do differently next time?	• Independent reflection • Action planning • Motivation to learn
What did you learn from another colleague today?	• Encouragement • Peer-based collaboration • Positive reinforcement • Self-concept
What is one takeaway from today that you are going to leave this training and tell someone else about today?	• Application • Motivation to learn • On-the-job application
What dots do you still need help connecting?	• Check for understanding • On-the-job application
What examples can you think of that demonstrate this concept?	• Check for understanding • Mining for practical examples
How will you apply this in the future? What specific steps can you take?	• Action planning • On-the-job application • Motivation to learn

What's Next?

As trainers and facilitators, we are continuous learners. We aim for more moments of self-actualization in our classroom, hoping to help our learners arrive at their own discoveries and even plan the mini parade to celebrate them when they do. More learner motivation! More ahas! More behavior change! As we aim for those light-bulb moments in our trainings, it requires us to take stock of what's working and what's not. It requires us to stretch beyond what we've been doing and encompass new approaches, to take risks, to challenge our own comfort, and potentially to shift our perspective in pursuit of the learning.

Invitation

To aim for impact, consider conducting audits at the conclusion of your next training program. This technique has you reflect on how effectively and frequently you demonstrated a skill and list its associated impact on the learners.

For example, Carrie often does question audits post-delivery (they are a continued focus for her) where she analyzes the questions she planned for versus the questions she delivered in the moment. She looks at patterns of question types (open, closed, round robin, fact-based, information seeking) and records the impact. Did the question lead to a new discovery? Did it divert the conversation? This approach allows you to examine what you planned, what you did, and why it mattered. This information can inform your next delivery.

Audits can be done with most facilitation skills, such as stories, examples, analogies, or activities. Choose a skill you're focusing on and conduct an audit using the following template.

Questioning Technique Audit

Course Name:

Course Date:

Participant Count:

Day	Question Count	Question Types	Barriers
Day 1 Morning	6	Application, information, round robin, overhead	Positive learning environment still being developed. In round robin, level of experience was not equipped to answer.
Day 1 Afternoon			
Day 2 Morning			
Day 2 Afternoon			

Stories/Examples/Analogies Audit

Course Name:
Course Date:
Participant Count:

Day	Stories	Result	Examples	Result	Analogies	Result
Day 1 Morning	Giraffe Story (Preferences)	+	Needs Assessment Example (Beauty Industry)	-	N/A	N/A
Day 1 Afternoon						
Day 2 Morning						
Day 2 Afternoon						

Chapter 7
Empathetic and Inclusive Facilitation

While *empathy* and *inclusion,* for some, might feel like buzzwords populating your LinkedIn feed and splashed across the cover of your favorite industry publication, these terms are rooted in several foundational theories that inform the talent development profession. We, the authors, agree that empathy and inclusion are not optional, but essential aspects of our role. For the purposes of this chapter, we are focusing on the specific skills to practice more empathetic and inclusive facilitation, spotlighting the role of the trainer and facilitator in influencing broader diversity, equity, and inclusion (DEI) organizational initiatives. We've also shared some resources at the end of the chapter for additional exploration of DEI initiatives more broadly.

So that we're starting off on the same page with definitions, here's how ATD's online glossary defines *diversity, equity,* and *inclusion:*

> **Diversity:** Diversity is the presence of differences that may include, but are not limited to, race, gender identity, sexual orientation, religion, ethnicity, nationality, socioeconomic status, language, physical or mental ability, and age. Diversity may also include differences in political perspective, learning preferences, personality, and communications preferences.
>
> **Equity:** Equity promotes justice, impartiality, fairness, and equal access to opportunities, advancement, and participation. Equity

addresses structural inequalities and barriers through fairness in procedures, processes, practices, and the distribution of resources. It differs from equality in that equality implies treating everyone as if their experiences and backgrounds are the same, whereas equity considers differences in people's experiences and backgrounds in determining what fairness looks like.

Inclusion: Inclusion means creating and fostering an environment in which everyone, including members of traditionally under-represented or marginalized groups, feels respected, welcome, and that they belong.

Adult Learning and Empathetic and Inclusive Facilitation

We introduced earlier Carl Rogers's learner-centered instruction and how it helped us all shift from a teaching mindset to a mindset where the learner and the facilitator are working equally. When Malcolm Knowles (1984) identified six key principles, he gave us further insights into the learner's need and moved adult learning theory into specific behaviors based on assumptions we can make about the uniqueness of adult learners. Knowles's adult learning principles are commonly used today to guide not only the delivery of content, but the design of outcome-based learning programs aimed at enhancing performance. They are also helpful in practicing empathetic and inclusive facilitation. Here's how these principles work in action (Table 7-1).

These principles tell us that adults learn best when they are motivated, when the content is relevant to their own experiences, and when they are presented with relevant examples and stories. You know who has relevant stories and examples? Every person in your training program. Their stories and examples not only matter but are essential to learning. A consistent piece of feedback we hear when facilitating ATD programs is that our participants embrace learning from their peers. The stories, examples, and tips shared among other talent development professionals in the room resonate, whether you're training on regulatory practices, DEI, management skills, or a new process for processing customer service tickets. Bring the stories into the training and invite every learner into the conversation.

Table 7-1. Adult Learning in Practice

Adult Learning Principle	Facilitation Skill
Know the Why: Adults need to know why something is important and relevant to them, their role, their organization, and their experience.	Conduct a prioritization activity at the start of the training asking learners to note their "why" for being in the training. What do they hope to walk out of the training knowing or knowing how to do better? Use this information to inform your approach to the content and be sure to explicitly link the content to someone's WIIFM (what's in it for me). Empathize with those who may not know their why or haven't had the opportunity to prioritize their why until this training.
Self-Directing: Adults need to direct their own learning experience and have choices for how they can learn.	Offer learners choice as often as possible. For instance, at the start of an activity, ask if they'd like to learn from new groups for the activity or stay in the groups they've already established. Offering a choice helps learners identify what they need to be successful and direct their own learning experience.
Life Experience: Adults need to draw on their own relevant examples and experiences to inform the learning and process new ideas.	Include learner-led discussions, storytelling, case studies, and source examples of applicability of key concepts from the learners themselves.
Readiness: Adults need to understand how the learning is relevant to their needs and how the learning will help them be ready to perform differently.	Help learners link lessons and activities to goals of the program and goals they've created for themselves (WIIFM). Empathize that one learner's journey in applying new skills on the job is likely different from their peers'.
Orientation: Adults need access to practical examples that are related to their on-the-job performance.	Learn who your learners are as individuals to consider examples, analogies, and stories that will help relate the content to the individuals in the room.
Self-Motivated: Adults are self-motivated and have a variety of internal motivating factors ranging from job security to self-esteem to satisfaction in their daily work.	Explore personalization and self-directed activities that empower the learner to explore the content creatively.

Whether your organization has a formal policy around DEI initiatives, you as a facilitator or trainer can lead by influence, paying attention to the things you can control in your learning program, your facilitation approach, and the language and approach you use to reach all learners.

What Is Empathetic Facilitation?

Whether you've viewed the *Inside Out* movie short that exemplifies empathy or read books by Brené Brown or Daniel Goleman, empathy permeates the talent development landscape. Empathy asks for a deep understanding of the problems and realities of others, or in this case those whose learning you are facilitating. Have you ever walked into a room and felt its energy, whether it was tense or excited or oozing indifference? Those with high empathy can walk into a space and feel the energy in the room in the same way most of us can walk into a room and feel the air as too cold. Empathetic facilitation is exercising learner-centered facilitation to its highest level. While being learner-centric is a logistical skill or task, empathy brings out the emotional facet of learning.

It's not just about getting learners to the center of the action, but how to get them to feel good about being there and make it a productive and equitable experience for all involved. It begins with practicing empathy as the facilitator and encouraging participants to empathize with one another as well. Maria Morukian explains how to practice empathy in her book *Diversity, Equity, and Inclusion for Trainers* (2022) by identifying two key practices we can focus on in training and delivery:

- **Compassion:** Practicing and modeling empathy and compassion for those who are different from us
- **Perspective taking:** Practicing and modeling curiosity, allowing all learners to hear the attitudes and behaviors of others

At times, it can be habit for us to think of our learners in terms of generalizations and statistics, but there's more to them than just their ages or job codes. Designing and delivering training with empathy means connecting with our learners, understanding their needs, and creating better learning experiences for them to engage in. That's where creating a realistic persona has power. So, go beyond the basics and include details like education, job experiences, motivations, the names of pets, and so forth. We even recommend including stock photos in your personas. These details may seem superfluous at first, but they're critical to bringing your personas to life. Fleshed-out personas feel like real people, and using them to guide your design and delivery process will make it easier for you to step into your learners's shoes.

It is important to note that truly equitable, accessible, and inclusive learning experiences begin at the needs assessment phase of design, when collecting goals, determining outcomes, and conducting needs analysis. And it continues into the design and development phase of designing learning, from using closed captioning to inclusive image selection. This is to say, it begins far before the implementation phase. However, as facilitators, it's our responsibility to equip ourselves with skills and perspectives that help us deliver equitable learning experiences (at least until the design is revisited with accessibility and inclusion in mind).

What Skills Make an Empathetic Facilitator?

Here are some of the tips for how you can begin to develop the skills you need to be an empathetic facilitator:

- **Perspective taking.** Understand a situation from the perspective of another person. In workplace learning, this means recognizing that application of new skills and knowledge on the job is unique for each individual.
- **Skills practice and scenarios.** In an exercise where you have participants who are experienced and those who are new, you might be inclined to allow the more experienced to work together and the less experienced to work together. But they could gain much by partnering together across experience levels and learning from each other's perspective.
- **Storytelling.** As facilitators, we have stories, relevant examples, and analogies that root the content in practicality. However, there are moments when we don't have the stories or, better yet,

our perspective in the story is not the one learners need to hear. Practice asking for an example from learners, but don't stop at one. Ask, "Is there an additional perspective we can consider, either similar or different?"

- **Demonstrating vulnerability.** We know to leverage the expertise in the room. If there is a learner with a master's degree in organizational psychology in the room, we won't facilitate the content around human performance improvement without consulting them to share their expertise.

- **Group dynamics.** How will you manage the dynamics of the group with an empathetic lens? Consider the unique individuality of each participant (and their learning motivations), observing participant engagement and behavior styles. Move throughout groups virtually or in person to observe participant interactions with one another and the content. Tip: Be careful of labeling a participant universally as having a particular behavioral style. Group dynamics are exactly that, *group* dynamics. If a learner in one group setting shows up analytical and observant and in another group session is more driving of the discussion, the key to their behavioral style lies in the interactions within the group.

Facilitation in Action

The Role of Facilities in Equitable Facilitation

Carrie was conducting a training for a group of 40+ individuals in a contracted training facility. As usual, she prepped for the training by sending detailed communications with the facility in advance and planning for the "what ifs," and as the training day approached, she thought she had all the bases covered. The training room she had been assigned was on the second floor of the building, and the only elevator on-site was an employees-only service elevator that required an employee escort and passcode to operate. Not only did Carrie not uncover this detail ahead of time, but she learned it was a challenge from a participant who didn't have the access they needed to the training room. As participants began arriving the morning of the training, Carrie knew she was missing one individual. Twenty minutes into the session, the learner walked into the session, after spending 30 minutes working with the facility to gain access to the service elevator. The result? An experience that was not equitable for this learner and left them feeling frustrated.

As the facilitator, Carrie had to use her empathy and inclusive mindset to address this oversight. She made adjustments in the moment to allow this individual time to get comfortable in the space once they'd arrived and turned the experience into a moment the entire group could learn from (especially because it was a train-the-trainer program). Carrie and the facility worked together at the first break in the program to create a structure for allowing ease of access to all participants for breaks, lunch, and arrival and departure times. Carrie had an empathetic conversation with the learner affected at the break, privately, to listen to their perspective.

Carrie, however, felt she had failed not only that individual but the rest of the learners. As a result, she examined her own bias and began considering new questions to ask of facilities that will uncover a variety of details for learners she may have previously overlooked. The question she added to her checklist of communications to facilities that had the most impact and continues to yield the most information: "What else do we need to consider that we aren't thinking of?" The question is open enough that the facilities's managers reply with everything from accessibility to food allergies to gender-neutral restrooms.

What Is Inclusive Facilitation?

Training delivery should include considerations around accessibility, gender-neutral vocabulary, jargon-free (and, yes, acronym-free) language, appropriate presentation of self, and attitudes about age, personal space, work, time, and reactions to authority (ATD 2019).

When we think about the facilitation techniques that help foster an inclusive environment, we might consider the icebreakers and energizers that we use throughout a program and the peer-based collaboration moments that allow for deeper discoveries in partnership with other learners.

The key to inclusive facilitation is ensuring everyone has the chance to participate in their own way. In the virtual classroom, this might look like providing options for response, such as, "Please respond how you are comfortable, either using the chat or by raising your hand and speaking to us directly." Or, in the in-person classroom, using a round-robin technique to hear from every individual in the room, showcasing an equitable space for contributions: "Let's hear a response from everyone to observe the variety of approaches we can take; as always, 'pass' is an option."

It is a recognition first that each program that we facilitate includes individuals from different backgrounds (education, socioeconomic, generation, expertise) and that each person is valued and has something to contribute to the learning experience. As facilitators, we should be conscious of creating an environment where everyone feels comfortable contributing.

Another key to inclusive facilitation is to start talking about inclusive facilitation by defining it for yourself and your organization. Pay attention to specific facilitation approaches and skills that we take as best practice and challenge them under the lens of inclusivity. Is there more you and your organization could be doing to prioritize inclusion in your learning events?

How Do I Ensure Facilitation Is Inclusive?

As facilitators, we play around in language most of the time. The content we facilitate is designed in a way that leverages rhetorical appeals (appealing to logic, credibility, or emotions) and devices to engage the learner. The way we present the content or introduce an activity is meant to make the learning accessible to every learner.

We can't pretend to know the preferences of each individual in the room when it comes to words that may render them passive or limit their capacity to learn in our classrooms. But we can invite them into the process of establishing parameters and guidelines for the learning to abide by.

Setting parameters for learning at the start of a session can have a profound impact on establishing a productive and comfortable learning environment. And they model inclusion and empathy while circumventing most challenges of the classroom before they happen, because they've been addressed at the outset.

We recommend allowing the learners in the room to set the parameters specifying what they need from one another. They are adults; they will tell you. Use the prompt, "What do we need from each other for this learning experience to be successful?" or "What do you need from me as your facilitator for this learning experience to be successful?" Once the parameters are defined by the group, record them somewhere (on a whiteboard, in participant workbooks, or on a wall chart) to return to when needed throughout the program.

Facilitation in Action

Inviting Learners to Share What They Need

Carrie applies an inclusive facilitation approach by inviting her learners to feel empowered to voice not only their needs but also their preferences for engagement, feedback, and interactions. In one learning program, with more than 28 participants in an in-person classroom, she and the learners began documenting on the back of their tent cards the things they needed from one another to have a successful learning experience. She asked them, "What do you need from each other to make this experience impactful?" Then she was silent.

She allowed the question to permeate, to really sink in and to invite them to tell one another, like the adult learners they were, exactly what they needed for learning to happen. The list on the back of the tent cards included needs relating to pronouns, sensitive words, and sensitivity to examples, rank, acronyms, and gender. The list was robust and informed a lot of how they worked together over the course of the program. Which, might we say, goes further than a slide with rules that have been predetermined for them to follow.

What Skills Make an Inclusive Facilitator?

It's a good question to ask yourself, your team, and your organization in an effort to formalize your focus on inclusive facilitation. Make it a practice to ask it often. It's not so much about acquiring new facilitation skills that make an inclusive facilitator but taking existing skills (questioning techniques, stories and examples, and ground rules) and reimagining them.

At ATD, we empower professionals across the globe to develop talent in the workplace, spanning a variety of industries and roles across the talent development landscape. Our approach to inclusive facilitation contains guidance around empathy, inclusive language, nonverbal cues, and guidelines for both the face-to-face and live online classrooms. And perhaps most important, it's an approach that is constantly evaluated, analyzed, and evolving.

Questioning techniques go beyond open- versus closed-ended questions and varying your questioning approach. Word choice in questioning typically contains bias in how we phrase questions, essentially "leading the witness," so to speak. For instance, "How much did we enjoy that activity?" implies learners should have enjoyed the activity and doesn't create space for those who didn't enjoy it to voice their perspective. The question to ask ourselves is, "Am I limiting the number of perspectives with my questions?"

We should also take a hard look at examples and analogies, which are frequently rich with cultural nuances and colloquialisms, and are heavily gendered. An inclusive facilitator also works to deliver feedback in a way that will be received by all participants, typically by opening with, "Are you open to feedback?" or "How do you best receive feedback?" In the next two sections, we'll tackle the language (verbal and nonverbal) we use in the classroom.

What Language Should I Look Out For?

The primary goal in using inclusive language is to reduce barriers that prevent individuals from learning, and to recognize that different words mean different things to different people. Language exists on a continuum, and as facilitators we want to consider how phrasing may exclude a learner from the conversation and eventually from the training as a whole. For example, nothing can make an individual feel like an outsider quicker than the use of three acronyms in one sentence. For instance, "The FOID model wasn't used properly by the IFT nor was it aligned with BACKCAD guidelines." Learners will inherently feel as if they should know something that they don't, and while some learners will ask for clarification, we want to ensure we include them without them requesting to be included. Try to avoid the use of acronyms when possible, and always explain them the first time they are used if they're unavoidable.

Gendered language can also go a long way toward making people feel excluded or misrepresented. Here are some tips on gendered language to be aware of:

- **You guys.** Etymology tells us that the term *guys* originated from the name of one man in history who attempted to assassinate King James I in 1605. Now it's a phrase used to casually address a group of individuals in American English, though many still consider it masculinized. There are several gender-neutral alternatives available as a replacement: *team, colleagues, everyone,* or *folks.*
- **Ladies and gentlemen.** Using gendered terms in your facilitation to address your learners can be alienating despite it feeling innocuous. Using collective "we" language can go a long way toward building a collaborative, team-based approach and including all who are present in the learning environment.
- **Pronouns.** Pronouns are often used to refer to an individual when not using their direct name. Pronouns are typically assumed, but there are lots of situations in which we can get them wrong—not just with trans or nonbinary learners, but with

people whose appearance is androgynous or gender noncon-forming according to our personal perception. Rather than assume, invite learners to share their pronouns, and if you get one wrong, apologize and move on. To this we add, model it before you claim it. For example, include your pronouns in your email signature, LinkedIn profile, or conferencing app iden-tifier. You can also open a session in a way that creates a safe space for others to do so, such as, "Good morning, my name is Nicole but you can call me Nikki. My pronouns are she/her. Let's go around the room and introduce ourselves as we'd like to be addressed today."

For Your Consideration

Generative Reflection

A key technique for assessing your facilitation approach is generative reflection (a fancy way of saying "Brainstorm what worked and didn't") at each break in the program, either in a scheduled break or at a moment when learners are applying new skills in an activity.

Here's how it works:

Jot down a list of words or phrases that you have used in your facil-itation, from memory if yours is sharp, or from reviewing a recording if you're at all like us and need to jog your memory. This allows you to cap-ture any words that you commonly use that stem from your own uncon-scious bias and your own geographically developed lingo, in addition to any stories or examples that stem from a place of unintentional exclusion or limited colloquialisms.

Be mindful that the word *accommodation* can be perceived as exclu-sionary. We are not offering something special or different to a learner; we are offering what each learner needs to be successful by providing equita-ble access to learning. Some examples:

▶ **Noninclusive Language:** "I think you're going to have a difficult time doing the teach-back activity."

- **Inclusive Language:** "How do you best participate when doing teach-back activities in a training program?"
- **Noninclusive Language:** "Perfect answer," "Thanks for the quick replies," "Amazing job," "Love that answer."
- **Inclusive Language:** "Thank you for sharing your thoughts with the group," "Celebrating that contribution because it links to our discussion on . . ."

Be mindful of using the following words during a conversation with a learner: *difficult, problem, challenge, different, disability, limited, limiting.* These words can project onto the learner's belief in their ability to succeed.

What Nonverbal Communication, Body Language, and Facial Expressions Do I Need to Be Aware Of?

What we don't say is equally as important as what we do say. If you've ever taken a course to develop your training and facilitation skills, body language is one of the key elements of good facilitation. We rely on rubric after rubric and checklist after checklist to tell us what good training delivery skills encompass, but what does that mean specifically? What used to be broad assumptions that applied in most cases are no longer serving the learners in our programs, and our body language might need to vary based on the participants in the room.

When we talk of body language, we think of stance, gestures, movement, facial expressions, and the myriad messages that these can communicate. Body language experts profess that as humans we are never in a state of not transmitting information to others. Our job is not to make assumptions or judgments but be open to accessing what a person is transmitting in a particular moment.

For Your Consideration

Mind Your Body Language

Former FBI agent and body language expert Joe Navarro (2019), who in his own words held the position of "catching spies," explains that body language is not about making judgments but accessing what a person is transmitting in a particular moment. For instance, when a learner crosses their arms, it's most likely a self-soothing behavior, not an attempt to block people out. In fact, in some cultures, crossing arms is a sign of respect and acceptance.

Erica Dhawan, author of *Digital Body Language: How to Build Trust and Connection, No Matter the Distance* (2021), explains that in our virtual worlds, "reading carefully is the new listening, and writing clearly is the new empathy. And a phone or video call is worth a thousand emails." Whether it's misinterpreted email replies, truncated Microsoft Teams messages, or videochats gone awry, the challenges stack up when it comes to effectively communicating through digital media.

To prepare for all the times we will be on camera in the virtual class-room or during in-person events, record your facilitation (we know, we know, it's moderately painful for most of us). In doing so you can iden-tify comfort behaviors (clasping your hands in front of your body) and restricted body cues (gestures that stay close to the body). More import-ant, bring your team (if you're lucky enough to have one) together in a room as an exercise in analyzing the facilitation together. What does your body language communicate to everyone and what nuances exist for each perspective?

What's a comfort behavior for you as a facilitator (clasping hands, hands crossed) and what does it signal to those in the room? A furrowed brow, a scrunched-up face, a tilted head, or pursed lips can present as hos-tile, intimidating, or judgmental to participants. Practice identifying what activates your comfort behavior—perhaps receiving a tough question or delivering content for the first time. Once you know when it happens, you can be prepared to substitute it for more inclusive body language to remain open for your learners.

How Can We Continue to Evolve What We Can't See Around Empathy and Inclusion?

We aim, as facilitators, to be curious, to take inventory of the field, and to commit to endless analysis of the ways trends and innovations shape the world, organizations, and the performance of individuals. This is often referred to as *future readiness*. But how do we plan for what we cannot see?

Readiness tells us that we must continually prepare for the unknown. So, we've shared some tips on how we stay ready for the change ahead.

- **Continue to embrace and model humility and openness.** It's hard to be accidentally inclusive; you must be intentional about it. As a facilitator, Jared wants to find out about people; he aims to be innately curious to find out what's going on in the learners's world culturally, regionally, organizationally, and personally because people bring that into the room with them. Checking everything at the door is a great concept but not realistic by any measure.

- **Engage in the conversation as best you can and seek out experts to learn from.** For Carrie, this means she speak to colleagues, mentors, learners, and those outside of the L&D landscape to take the pulse of where we as a society are moving. And she truly looks to the learners to engage with them about what they are seeing in their own organizations, aiming to remain innately curious. She's also a lover of stories. She wants to illuminate every single story, and so she remains committed to doing that with each learner she encounters.

What Are Some Activities for Building Empathy and Inclusion?

Energizers and icebreakers are typically woven throughout a training program, used at the facilitator's discretion when learners need an increase in energy (energizers) or familiarizing (icebreakers). While energizers and icebreakers can feel like an overtly playful (and sometimes silly) additive to the seriousness of learning (a former participant's words, not ours), they can be quite impactful and informative. Especially if we tailor them to build inclusion and empathy.

If done well, the icebreakers and introductions that you use at the start of a training program can go a long way toward building empathy among your learners. This approach models empathetic facilitation from the outset of a program and shows everyone in attendance that you, as the facilitator, prioritize the learners's context, point of view, and motivation for learning. Strong introductory activities are incredibly impactful when you can help learners connect the dots between their context and motivation and the content being covered in the training.

As facilitators, we link learners' interests to the content and help them see the benefit of the learning experience. When that's done well, there's no battle to be fought in bringing them along; they are instead lining up to walk alongside us.

To build empathy in your training programs, try the following:

Activity 1

The Situation
The learners are showing signs of fatigue in the afternoon of an all-day training. You know they are tired from the morning session and nervously anticipating the end-of-day skills practice activity.

The Trick
Use continuum lines to demonstrate the varying elements or approaches to a content-specific question.

How It Works
Ask the learners to place themselves on the continuum (in person or live online) in response to your question. For instance, if you're facilitating a training on effective feedback, you may have them line up on one side of the continuum if the last time they delivered effective feedback was in the last week and the other end of the continuum if it was more than six months ago. Not only do you as the facilitator gain insight into learners' familiarity and experience level with the topic, but they are aware of their own and their peers's responses.

For the virtual classroom, this can be a whiteboard activity with a line drawn across the whiteboard with the annotation tool. Have the learners place their cursor or type their initials on the continuum to show where they would place themselves.

Pro Tip

The question you use for the continuum can be intentional and topical, or it can be used as an energizer that allows a learner's full personality to be present in the space. For example, ask, "Are you a night owl or an early bird?" Once they've placed themselves on the continuum, ask a follow-up question, such as, "For those of you who are night owls, what do you need in a learning experience?" This will allow each group to frame their experience for the other group to understand and empathize with.

Activity 2

The Situation

"The brain doesn't pay attention to boring things," as we know from John Medina's book, *Brain Rules* (2008). You're finishing a 20-minute lesson that is mostly lecture and has rendered the learners passive. The next activity is designed to be independent reflection, but you know the group needs something more interactive.

The Trick

Leverage playful discovery and experimentation, an accelerated learning principle, to enhance the learning process by using physical activity, creativity, music, images, color, and other methods designed to get people deeply involved in their own learning. Playful discovery unlocks much of our potential for learning that has been left largely untapped by most conventional learning methods. Accelerated learning principles center on how we acquire knowledge. Here we'll skew playful discovery toward an activity aimed at building empathy among learners.

How It Works

Post wall charts around the room and have learners grab a marker and stand by a chart of their choosing. Ask them to draw what they want their next year to look like (encourage visuals only). For virtual learning, you can use the whiteboard feature. When everyone is done, facilitate a share-back where learners explain their drawing. When we did this for a team-work and relationship-building session, we also asked, "What can we do to help make this happen?" For learners who are not on a team together, that question could be changed to, "What would support you making this happen?" to identify possibilities and potentially generate empathy from their fellow learners.

Pro Tip
This activity can be modified for time restrictions and small groups by conducting it in partnered pairs.

Activity 3

The Situation
You are facilitating a training program with the C-suite, and when facilitating training programs or meetings with the C-suite, it's important—just as with other audiences—to break the ice and get everyone ready to participate. At the same time, you shouldn't approach learners with activities that they won't take seriously; rather, invite them into something meaningful.

The Trick
If your icebreakers make the training event seem fun and silly before everyone is comfortable, executives may see the whole thing as a waste of time, affecting the energy of your program. Senior leaders expect efficiency and purpose, so you should let these expectations drive how you design introductory activities for them.

How It Works
The icebreaker Throw It Out can be especially useful when you want learners to let go of the doubts or preoccupations they may bring into the learning space. It encourages them to open their minds, which makes it effective for dealing with change management topics. Here's how it works:

1. At the start of your program, after walking through your agenda for the time together, ask participants to take a sticky note off the table and write down any hesitations they have about the training program or why the change that the training program addresses won't work. This is for their eyes only.
2. Open the door to the classroom, then have participants wad up their notes and throw them outside the door.
3. Close the door and ask that your learners leave what they wrote outside—at least until the end of the day. Tell them that it's OK to go outside and pick up their notes after class, but until then they are encouraged to focus on what positive things can come out of the time spent inside.

Pro Tip

You can easily modify Throw It Out to work during a session when participants need to come to a resolution, too. Simply change what you ask participants to write down. In a resolution-driven meeting, for example, you might ask participants to throw out the obstacles that will prevent them from accomplishing the meeting's goals. In the virtual classroom, invite participants to add their thoughts to a whiteboard and let those thoughts stay on that whiteboard (be sure to save it and bring it back to your final session). Or, consider using a polling application to populate their obstacles in a word cloud.

To build inclusion in your training programs, try the following:

Activity 4

The Situation

As a trainer, it's easy to get into a pattern of relying on the more energized or extroverted participants. Or perhaps you have a participant who likes to offer a joke at every available opportunity. How can we as facilitators give other participants a chance to contribute to the conversation without obviously shutting out louder voices?

The Trick

Rather than defaulting to learners who have their hands raised to answer a question, create a structure for calling on others. This will make for a more inclusive discussion and lead to increased engagement.

How It Works

As part of your preparation in the face-to-face classroom, place stickers— colored dots, fruit icons, or other types of decals (for example, stars or slogans)—on learners' name tents, participant guides, or the backs of chairs in a random fashion.

When the time arrives for a debrief or to solicit input from participants, rather than having learners raise their hands, tell the class that you want to hear from those who, for example, have an apple sticker. This enables introverts who may need a moment to gather their thoughts to participate more actively. It will also put that eager participant on notice that they should allow other voices into the room. (If you've put the stickers on the backs of chairs, this is an opportunity to get participants up and out of their chairs for a moment. Because many learners aren't cognizant that the stickers are present, it also adds an element of surprise.)

For the virtual classroom, display a slide that has various images of food, beverages, animals, and candy on it and ask participants to select their "prize." When it's time to debrief an activity or engage learners in discussion, you can call on specific prizes and invite those individuals to contribute.

Pro Tip

You don't need to call on individuals by sticker color or type for every question; you can mix this in with the usual hand raising. But using the trick can add new perspectives, help introverts gain new confidence, and overcome challenging behaviors.

Activity 5

The Situation

At the start of a session, you want to build empathy, inclusion, and a positive group dynamic. Your learners are mildly familiar with one another but don't have a lot of overlap in their roles.

The Trick

Conduct an intentional activity that builds empathy with the learners and is rooted in the objectives of the training program or the content topic itself.

How It Works

Get an inflatable beach ball or sports ball. Write questions on each section of the ball. Lead a ball-toss activity where each person tosses the ball gently to another learner. When they catch the ball, they answer the question that their thumb lands on.

For the virtual classroom, you can allow a learner to select whom to pass to; when the next person is selected, they can unmute (and perhaps come on camera) and share.

Pro Tip

Center the questions on the ball on the topic of the training. For instance, in a conflict resolution training, the ball had thought-provoking questions that allowed participants to share how they deal with conflict. The responses drove discussions and gave people opportunities for perspective taking. They were sharing stories and answers to the questions, which naturally led to additional questions and conversations throughout the training.

What's Next

While we are not experts in the DEI space, empathetic and inclusive facilitation is a constant focal point for us as a facilitator team. We've compiled a list of trusted experts and resources that we turn to when expanding our knowledge of DEI that we're passing along to you in this chapter's invitation. The key for us is to continually focus on the unique position we are in as facilitators to influence change in this space and model best practices.

Invitation

Start somewhere. Anywhere. Just begin. Start a conversation, read an article, share a podcast, ask a question. To get you started, we've listed experts who are leading the conversations around empathy, inclusion, and DEI efforts both inside and outside the talent development landscape.

Resources to Get Started:

- Read the *TD at Work* issue "Prioritize Inclusivity in Your Training," by Eliza Blanchard. We are deeming this a must-read for any facilitator.
- The ATD DE&I Podcast Series explores DEI topics with special guests across the talent development function.
- Add Maria Morukian's book *Diversity, Equity, and Inclusion for Trainers* to your toolkit.
- Take a course on DEI, such as ATD's DEI in Talent Development Certificate Program.
- Read or listen to Erica Dhawan's book *Digital Body Language*.
- Read or listen to Brené Brown's book *Dare to Lead*.
- Watch Disney's *Inside Out* and bring some popcorn and candy.
- Read Maureen Orey's "The Many Aspects of Accessibility," chapter 23 in *ATD's Handbook for Training and Talent Development,* 3rd Edition.
- Check out anything written by Daniel Goleman, and specifically his book *Working With Emotional Intelligence.*
- Take a free course to learn about digital accessibility, such as this one offered by the Accessibility Initiative: w3.org/WAI/fundamentals/foundations-course.

Chapter 8
The Art of Feedback

Feedback is the flow of information from one person to another about how useful or successful a process, a behavior, or an action is (ATD 2019). During any training or talent development program, learners need to receive feedback regarding their progress to help with their behavioral change. This means we need to understand the feedback techniques that help participants in our programs see whether they are learning and progressing.

However, in a *Harvard Business Review* article, Marcus Buckingham and Ashley Goodall (2019) spotlight that "more than 50 percent of your rating of someone reflects *your* characteristics, not [theirs]." They also point out that neuroscience tells us that our fight or flight response is triggered by feedback that can inhibit our ability to learn new things. So how can we as facilitators do feedback a little differently, in a way that doesn't inhibit learning?

If, as Buckingham and Goodall suggest, neuroscience shows "learning rests on our grasp of what we're doing well, not what we're doing poorly," then imagine engineering a switch in your brain that allows you to focus on the strengths and unique value of an individual learner each time you deliver feedback. This isn't to say constructive feedback can't be provided. It's to say we can help them see how the feedback can be applied to them specifically and leveraged for growth; we can even involve them in how they'd like to receive feedback.

In chapter 1, we spoke of the facilitator's mindset and how a growth mindset can influence how we show up and contribute to a learning experience. That conversation carries over into our discussion around feedback.

Feedback can get a bad reputation in training programs, oftentimes because it misses the mark. Either it's vague and unclear ("you have great energy" or "great effort"), or it can feel like a personal or professional attack ("your sarcastic nature makes others shut down when learning"). You'll notice that as we explore feedback in our role as trainers throughout this chapter, we give you considerations that will help challenge your thinking or shape your perspective on feedback. We honor that there are varying approaches to feedback in training programs and among experts in the field of feedback—many of whom we've included in this chapter. We recommend you turn to them for a deeper cognitive understanding of the art of feedback.

The Art of Feedback

We receive feedback all day, every day, in various formats and from a variety of sources, including the technology we use, the relationships we foster, and the bodies we inhabit. It could be your fitness tracker telling you to stand up and move because you have been sitting for too long, your partner telling you that the coffee you made that morning was a touch too bitter, or that small ache in your lower back telling you something's stiff every time you bend over too far. Feedback is a broad and sweeping category, but for the purposes of our discussion we'll be exploring:

- How we give feedback to our learners
- How we manage feedback in our learning programs
- How we receive feedback on our performance as a trainer

According to Harvard professors and feedback experts Sheila Heen and Douglas Stone (2014), receiving feedback sits directly at the intersection of two conflicting human desires: acceptance and growth, which begins to uncover why feedback can be so challenging to receive well. Their latest book, *Thanks for the Feedback: The Science and Art of Receiving*

Feedback Well, explores this intersection and identifies three various forms of feedback: appreciation, coaching, and evaluation.

This chapter allows us to explore the various facets of feedback—giving it and receiving it—focusing on how feedback can guide our performance as trainers. Some pieces of the feedback puzzle are easier to navigate than others, but they all come together to help our programs, our learning experiences, our learners, and ourselves reach our fullest potential.

Why Is Feedback So Hard?

Your feedback narrative is any experience, thought, or belief that has formed your perspective on feedback. What is your physiological reaction to feedback? Does your skin flush when receiving feedback? Do you shift your stance when feedback is delivered? Do you break eye contact? Do you get defensive? Are you just not in the mood? It's important to assess your own assumptions, beliefs, and biases when it comes to feedback to understand how that might be swaying how you give and receive feedback in your learning programs.

Here's what we came up with.

Jared grew up as a dancer, and in the dance world there is constant feedback: feedback from your body when you fall out of a turn, feedback from the instructor to point your toe, or feedback from a partner when you are out of sync. Once he reached the corporate world, he was expecting feedback in the moment and often, as he had experienced in the dance world. The difference: He was having to continually ask for feedback in the workplace. When he delivers feedback in his training programs, Jared finds opportunities during activities and in the flow of the course to deliver instantaneous feedback to allow learners to continue practicing with the feedback in mind.

Carrie grew up on a nationally competitive athletic team where feedback was blunt, direct, and delivered at a time when she least expected it. She grew comfortable receiving feedback, but more in the form of start-and-stop feedback. Start doing this. Stop doing this. Clear, direct, and no blurry spaces in between. Now, when receiving feedback that is riddled with blurry spaces, she is left sometimes feeling frustrated with its vagueness (something she's always working on growing from). When she delivers feedback in her training programs, she begins by asking if the learner is open to feedback before offering it to ensure they are willing and open to receiving the feedback. She also uses a coaching approach by providing clear feedback on what happened and the impact it had, and then engaging the learner with a question centered on what they would do differently next time.

What is your feedback narrative? What has informed your viewpoint on feedback?

_____

_____

For Your Consideration

Facilitation Can Improve Feedback

A Gallup workplace survey on feedback found that only 26 percent of employees strongly agree that the feedback they receive helps them do better work (Wigert and Dvorak 2019). Too often in the workplace, feedback is given as a one-way delivery vehicle to address performance challenges or evaluate performance. In recent years, the understanding and application of feedback in the workplace has evolved with a surge in coaching and mentoring approaches as well as more frequently cadenced feedback conversations to begin normalizing feedback conversations. So, we've come a long way and there's a lot of rewiring our brains around feedback to be done. As trainers and facilitators, we have a unique position in normalizing and redefining effective feedback in our learning programs to impact individuals and the organization.

What Models Can I Use to Deliver Feedback During My Learning Programs?

When we are giving feedback, there are many models to consider. Depending on the type of program you're facilitating and your organizational perspective on feedback, you may need to adjust. We are not advocating for one model over another when it comes to giving feedback as much as we are advocating for familiarity of what exists and an openness to make a model your own when practicing giving feedback. Get ready for some acronyms:

- Situation-Behavior-Impact (SBI) Model
- Behavior, Example, Effect, Future (BEEF) Model
- Action, Impact, Development (AID) Model
- Behavior Impact Future Feelings (BIFF) Model
- Pendleton's Feedback Model
- Situation/Task, Action, Result (STAR) Model
- Describe, Express, Specify, Consequences (DESC) Model

What these models have in common is they move the feedback-giver through a linear process of what happened and the result of that action. Some models pay more deference to feelings and inputs from the recipient of the feedback, and some spend more time focusing on specificity. When it comes to using a model in training programs, it's a matter of practicing using the models and involving your learners in the process.

In ATD's Training & Facilitation Certificate Program and ATD Master Trainer Program, feedback from peers and the facilitator is integral to the learner experience. When leveraging peer-based feedback, the parameters and boundaries for that feedback need to be clearly stated and agreed upon, including both how to give feedback and how to receive feedback. Once the parameters are established, the facilitator can tailor their approach based on the needs of the learner. Let's look at an example.

The feedback model used in our train-the-trainer program focuses on constructive feedback using the following model that was developed to align to the course outcomes:

- The learner (receiver of the feedback) shares three pieces of feedback reflecting on their own performance (two positive and one opportunity or developmental area).
    - Note the intentional usage of *opportunity* or *developmental area* instead of *negative*—words matter.

- The peer group shares their feedback, providing at least one constructive feedback statement and aiming for no repeated feedback.
- The learner (receiver of the feedback) can respond to feedback in two ways: with a clarifying question or a "thank you."

Facilitation in Action

Adapting Feedback Techniques to Your Learners

In her programs, Carrie tailors this feedback model to the learners in the room, ensuring that the feedback is organizationally aligned. For instance, during a train-the-trainer program with 36 participants, the feedback model was offered to guide their experience. The learners were new to training, and when polling them on day one for the what's in it for me (WIIFM), she noticed that more than two-thirds of the group wrote down "build my confidence" (or a variation of that sentiment). Confidence was a main driver for the group, so the model worked well to ensure they started by reflecting on their own performance and reprogramming themselves to start with the positive (sounds easy enough, but most trainers will inevitably begin with what went wrong or what wasn't quite right).

In another group of learners, the experience level of each was 10 or more years of training delivery, and the group was looking to hone and elevate existing skills. When Carrie presented the feedback guidance described earlier, a learner immediately spoke up to offer a different approach. "I like this approach and see the benefit of it," they began. "But, for me, I just want straight and to-the-point feedback. I don't want to mess around with the fluff. Clear and concise is what we'll do back on the job." The collective nods and comments from the rest of the group confirmed this suggestion. Carrie needed to account for possibly shifting the feedback approach to meet the needs of the learners to replicate how they'd give and receive feedback on the job, while still maintaining the integrity of the approach for any learner who may not be speaking up. She polled the group, allowing them to select the feedback model they'd like to use.

All the learners voted for the latter approach suggested by the learner. With that, Carrie posed an important question: "What structure do we want to build for the feedback with this new approach in mind?" While honoring the request to tailor the feedback to meet the experience and needs of the learners, Carrie ensured the collective group still created a structure to follow. This not only ensured consistency in giving and receiving feedback and that each learner walked away with the same inputs from their peers, but it allowed them to think through their approach intentionally. And in the end, they created a clear and concise feedback model but kept the first step, where they analyzed their own performance.

How Do I Give Effective Feedback During My Learning Programs?

Let's begin with accepting that effective feedback for you may not be effective feedback for one of your learners. Similarly, each learner will receive the same feedback differently. Offering feedback to participants during instruction is essential for their growth and development of new knowledge, skills, and attitudes, so determining how to deliver that feedback effectively is key. Without feedback in learning programs, learners are left wondering, "Did I hit the mark?" or "Did I meet expectations?" or "Did I learn what I needed to learn?"

In ATD programs, we encourage participants to give one another actionable feedback focusing on what the observed action or behavior was, specific feedback that the learner can act on, and the impact the observed action or behavior has.

For example, "When I saw you use eye contact during your skills presentation, I noticed it made the learner feel prepared to be called on. Please keep doing this in the future." Or, "What I observed was that you did not use participants' names. Try starting with the name and then asking the person the question." Like learning objectives, our feedback should be specific and actionable.

There are various tips for delivering effective feedback to learners, but we've called out some here:

- **Engage the learner to provide self-directed feedback.** Ask your learners for their thoughts first on what went well in each situation and what they could improve before sharing feedback. This requires a coaching approach to feedback, and many times we observe the learner self-reflecting and providing themselves the feedback that we were going to supply.
- **Ask the learner how they would like to receive feedback.** This approach uses feedback to begin a conversation, not a monologue, by gaining partnership from the learner to enter into the feedback conversation. Adult learners can tell you what they need to be successful.
- **Consider when feedback should be given.** Should the feedback be given in real time or in a follow-up feedback conversation? There are benefits to each and it may depend on individual preferences. If it is more general feedback, you could provide it in real time. If it is more specific and individualized, maybe sending them a heads-up about the feedback conversation would be best so that you can use that time to be specific and direct.
- **Use the technique of global feedback.** Global feedback is feedback that applies to the whole group. This can be a good strategy to supplement peer-based feedback and focus the group of learners. For example, you could say, "I noticed when I was observing your presentations that many of you went over time. Consider cutting down your presentations in length when possible." Or, "When you're facilitating instructions to an activity, ensure you are clear and direct. I heard a lot of narration about what you were going to start doing instead of getting us started in the activity."

Try some of our favorite methods:

- Share one thing they should start doing, one thing they should stop doing, and one thing they should keep doing. This is known as Start-Stop-Keep.

- Share performance details that wowed you and performance suggestions or considerations framed as "How about you try this." This is known as Wow and How About.
- Don't wait for dedicated moments in the learning program to offer structured feedback. Consider offering feedback frequently to help normalize the giving and receiving of feedback throughout the program.
- Offer feedback learners can act on, and check for clarity.

What Are Some Situations When I'd Need to Deliver Feedback?

Feedback in learning programs comes in many shapes and sizes: verbal, written, self-assessment, peer-to-peer, game scores, and exam results, to name a few. We provide feedback as part of debriefing activities, critiques of observations or role plays, corrections to incorrect responses, and adjustments when simulated experiences don't go 100 percent to plan.

The range of feedback also depends on the formality of the assessment. Let's think of this as how we measure progress and learning during the training event to ensure that our learners are getting what they need, and ultimately put them on the right track to improve performance back on the job.

There are times when a situation in a learning program may require in-the-moment, direct feedback. Let's look at an example:

> **The Situation:** Xavier (they/them) is oversharing. They are energized, engaged, experienced, and enthusiastic (all the "E's") to share their ideas and suggestions with the larger group. They are continuing to dominate the large group conversations as well as some small group activities. You observe passive behavior from other learners and read their body language signals to determine that Xavier's behavior is compromising the learning. As the trainer, you know you need to advocate for the larger group and give feedback to this learner to free up some space that allows others to contribute to the learning experience.

You have a few options when it comes to giving feedback. As you review the options, which do you think will have the most impact for this learner and, more important, why?

- **Option A:** "Maurice, I notice you are excited to share with everyone your experiences. It is fantastic that you have so much knowledge and wisdom."
- **Option B:** "Maurice, I noticed you are raising your hand frequently. Are you OK if we hear from someone else to gain their perspective?"
- **Option C:** "Let's hear from someone we haven't heard from yet."

Is there an option that resonates with you? (Go ahead and place a star next to the option you prefer.) What do you notice about the differences in the language used in each of these responses? Which would you be most comfortable saying in front of a group? Which one got to the point fastest?

You may have noticed that as you progress through options A, B, and C, we move from providing validation for the learner (option A), to asking and seeking permission from the learner (option B), to telling the learner directly what we expect to happen (option C). Again, there is no right or wrong approach, but our stance is that option C is both direct and models inclusivity.

How do we get to the point of reaching option C with our learners? First, ask yourself, have I established a positive learning environment? If the foundation has been built, then achieving option C is easier to obtain. The best way to quickly get to this point is to model what we expect ourselves, and then the learners tend to follow suit when it comes to giving feedback to us as trainers as well as to one another.

Second, ask yourself, have I established group commitments or best practices for how we can learn together? If expectations for optimum learning have been at addressed at the start of the program, those expectations will guide our feedback. Consider inputting a feedback-oriented question into the best practices and expectation-setting conversation of how the group will both give and receive feedback so it does not come as a surprise. Use phrases like, "Here is what good looks like," "These are our best practices," or "This is how you will be evaluated."

Here are some other situations that you may experience in the classroom, and what feedback looks like for each. As you review the examples, consider what you have used before in terms of feedback methods and what you could try in future sessions.

Discussion Board

Say you are working on a blended learning program on the topic of financial awareness. The learners must complete asynchronous content before making their way to the live synchronous portion of the program. The program requires the learners to respond to conversation prompts on a discussion board as part of this preparation.

Before delivering feedback, you review the comments posted on the discussion board and check for clarity, correctness, and quality. You respond to the learners' comments and questions with constructive advice, examples, and practical experiences. This not only acknowledges their work but also provides them with learning guidance before heading into the synchronous event.

Electronic Poll

You have created an online poll with knowledge check questions from the previous sessions' content using polling software (such as Slido, Mentimeter, or Poll Everywhere). The learners reply with their best guesses, and the results reveal that the learners are not trending in line with the correct responses and seem confused as they review the results.

Your feedback might sound like this: "Ah, team, we seem to have quite a range of responses with these results. It looks like we may need to dig in deeper to a few of these topics. Which question would you like to look at first?" This opens the dialogue for the learners to be in control of where the discussion goes in terms of what support they need most.

Wow and How Abouts

You have finished day one of three all-day training sessions on coaching techniques and are looking for learners to provide you feedback on the course experience. Overall, you thought the activities and flow of the program went well. You ask the group, as their "ticket" out for the day, to describe either a "Wow" (something that went well, like the role-play activity) or a "How About" (something that could be improved, like, "Can we share more of our own experiences tomorrow?"). In the classroom, this feedback can be left on a wall chart and, in the virtual classroom, it can be added in private chat or on a whiteboard.

You can take the evening to reflect on the feedback left at the end of the day. Based on the responses, you can check in with the group in the morning to suggest adjustments, saying, "Team, I understand that you liked the role-play activity; can we add in another one of those to practice crucial conversations today?" This approach allows you to take the learner feedback and implement it accordingly, increasing engagement, and it allows you to model how to receive and adapt to feedback.

Challenging Situations and Behaviors

In chapter 5, we discussed techniques for managing challenging situations and tips for overcoming challenging behaviors, but it's worth mentioning here as well. Challenging behaviors from learners in our programs are in fact feedback for us to take in. Challenges are information about what's working, what's not working, and what may be affecting one learner, which can inadvertently have impacts on other learners and the overall learning experience. When a challenge occurs in the flow of the learning that could potentially compromise the learning outcomes, we are required to receive the feedback the challenge may be giving us. Then, we must plan to overcome it by delivering feedback to an individual learner or the entire group. On our facilitator team, we aim to focus on overcoming a challenging *behavior* while not managing the *participant* exhibiting the behavior (again, note the subtle semantic shift of *managing* versus *overcoming*).

Facilitation in Action

Leveraging Feedback in Activities

A recent program Darryl facilitated culminated with participants doing a practical application of what they learned by completing a brief 10-minute skills demonstration. They were encouraged to create an interactive presentation with visual elements. It was an excellent way of assessing whether learners picked up on the key ideas and concepts covered during the program.

With the 10-minute time constraint, most of the learners completed the skills demonstration using a wall chart or slide deck to aid the learning. However, one learner in the program took a fun and calculated risk to model some of the interactive learning methods they discovered during the program. To present their content, the learner designed a trivia game using the Kahoot app.

They then placed tape on the floor, creating three rows, and instructed participants to arrange themselves along the tape lines. Whenever the participants got a correct answer, they could take a step up in their row; if they got an incorrect answer, they had to take one step back. The participant who got closest to the finishing line at the end of the trivia game was declared the winner and awarded a prize.

While the Kahoot app visually provides the same elements of participant progress and prizes for winning, the learner took a risk to make their game more interactive, and demonstrated an understanding of the key concept covered in the program of taking action to reach learners.

When learners get to demonstrate their learning by showcasing their skills to other learners, there's an opportunity for feedback. Feedback post-activity should be given to the learners to make them aware of whether their performance hit the mark. For more informal activities, it could be a reflection activity, a discussion, or peer-to-peer critiques. For higher-level activities, feedback may be more formal, and one-on-one coaching may occur depending on the outcome. Again, in both instances,

> observable and measurable examples should be given to the learners to allow them to grow from the feedback.

How Do I Receive Constructive Feedback as the Facilitator and Use It for Growth in My Performance?

Let's switch gears from the feedback we provide our learners to the feedback we receive about our performance as trainers and facilitators via post-course evaluations or similar methods. Receiving feedback is how we know how to keep doing facilitation behaviors that are working and minimize behaviors that are not serving our learners. This includes opportunities throughout the learning program (formative feedback) and opportunities at the conclusion of the learning program (summative feedback).

Formative Feedback

When we request feedback, we want to be intentional when seeking it. Why do we want it? What purpose is it going to serve? It all starts with building a positive learning environment. If the learners feel safe, the feedback is more likely to come in. If we as trainers let our guard down a bit, we are more willing to be vulnerable.

For example, Nikki builds trust with her learners as part of the best practices of every program. She requests that the learners provide continual feedback throughout the program and creates a space for the feedback to flow. She asks learners to share how her facilitation could be modified to adapt to their needs, how she could vary the instructional methods used, or how to modify an approach. Continual feedback allows adaptions to be made for the learners and models inviting feedback. This sounds like, "Let's have open communication throughout our program. Tell me if I need to slow down or repeat something in the moment it occurs. I want to maximize the learning experience and ensure that it is meeting your needs. Can I get your commitment in that?"

When it comes to receiving feedback, aim to not take it too personally. As the receiver of the feedback, you choose how you'd like to process that information and what you'd like to do with it. One time Nikki received this feedback on her slide deck for a conference session: "I did not appreciate the motion animations and colors in the slide deck." That was just one comment from an audience member. Other comments glowed about the audience experience, but Nikki's initial reaction was to process how she could change the entire slide deck for next time. And then she paused. She realized that was one perspective, while no one else had commented on that. She decided to try it again before making revisions. She also considered how some colors are not clearly discernible to all learners and researched the accessibility of motion animations.

Summative Feedback

Post-course surveys allow learners to provide feedback on the course by measuring the content, the facilitator (and producer for live online), and the overall experience. ATD uses post-course survey data to inform each delivery and equips our facilitator team with access to those surveys. The survey data and comments serve as a feedback conversation to examine opportunities for improvement.

A great example is when Carrie first joined ATD. Her evaluations hit the benchmark in terms of overall score for facilitating the program, but upon further analysis of learner comments and patterns across programs, she realized she was consistently rated lowest in her performance on providing relevant stories and examples. As she reviewed each delivery, she noticed that feedback was a constant theme. Her first response was to audit how many stories and examples she was using in the program to evaluate and potentially modify her preparation. What she found was that she was using stories and examples, but learner feedback revealed they were lacking. With continued analysis and the support of discussions with her facilitator team, she began to realize it wasn't that she wasn't telling stories and using examples; she wasn't doing it effectively. She needed to change her approach.

Carrie's new approach involved planning for the type of story she'd use to ground the content in practical application, and then tailoring it to her audience. Perhaps a group of learners in the healthcare industry needed different examples for the material to resonate, or a manufacturing team would need to hear different aspects of her stories than a group of learners in sales. The feedback allowed her to hone her approach to meet learner needs.

Now, our ATD facilitator team includes post-course evaluation analysis as a regular part of the preparation process for future programs. Integrating it into our pre- and post-course process ensures the learners's feedback is reviewed, considered, and leveraged as the gift that it is. We operate under the belief that feedback is welcomed, necessary, and always received (even when it's hard, and it can get really hard).

What if I'm in a Role Where Feedback Is My Only Performance Metric?

We have the experience as facilitators of pouring our heart and soul into the preparation process and supporting our learners throughout the learning experience. So when our main form of how well we did is measured by a five-question quick pulse survey of learners's reactions, it can feel like only part of the story. Sometimes we get the benefit of detailed learner comments to provide rationale, but sometimes we don't. Sometimes these scores are passed along to other departments, colleagues, and managers, and we want to yell in the hallways, "That's not the whole story," to truly showcase our value to the organization. Does one low score mean we are underperforming? What if it was an off day? Or the learner was frustrated with the content and not the facilitator?

When your role is mostly tied to subjective survey scores, you can consider what other metrics you are going to use to showcase your performance. Here are some tips for soliciting feedback on your performance:

- Invite someone to audit your facilitation. Ask them to focus on particular topics or pose questions to them to guide their responses (you'll get more detailed feedback this way).
- Audit your own work (via video or audio) to highlight areas of growth over time.
- Conduct pre- and post-assessments of your performance, setting up measurable behaviors and examples to demonstrate your growth.
- Collect learner feedback throughout the program in a place you can return to (we use a trusty Microsoft Word document—nothing fancy needed). This will allow you to remember what's working and what's not in your programs over an extended period of time instead of one instance.

The key is setting guidelines via a rubric to indicate success. For example, you may ask an auditor to watch specifically for your questioning techniques to ensure that you use a variety of question types (such as four different types per 60-minute time block). This approach will measure if you have achieved that mark by having the outside observer note it. You can then articulate to stakeholders the impact that your improved performance had on learners and the learning event.

If you're in a role where performance feedback is your only metric, consider partnering with learners as well as their managers and supervisors to find touchpoints to receive informal feedback that tells the broader story of your impact.

How Do I Move Past the Poor Feedback I Might Receive?

Facilitator evaluations can leave us feeling reduced to a number, and let's be honest, they can evoke some pretty strong feelings. And when it comes to evaluative feedback, feelings are hard. Evaluation scores are data that contribute to the story of our impact; they are not the whole story. Sometimes it's about inferring what was meant, demystifying the comment threads, or understanding what we can take away from a facilitator rating of 1 out of 5 (ouch!). If you receive evaluation scores after your training delivery, we suggest not looking at them instantly. (Easier said than done, we know.)

Some of us are better at that than others; for instance, Darryl likes to reflect on his experience facilitating and the learners he interacted with before reviewing scores, sometimes waiting until a week later. Other facilitators (ahem, Carrie) may rush to review the evaluation almost immediately, eager to get a sense of validation or understanding of what impact the program had on a particular group.

Take a moment to pause and reflect on the experience yourself first. Separate the class and the evaluations with a few days. This can allow you time to digest the comments and scores with a clearer, more objective mind in reading the responses. Look for common phrases or words and analyze the data and comments to identify one area you'd like to focus on in your next delivery. And lastly, harness a growth mindset and look at your evaluation feedback as information to inform your next performance, thinking of what new thing you will try to yield a different result.

Facilitation in Action

Get Creative on Gathering Feedback to Prove Impact

One tactic Nikki uses is reaching out to learners 30 days after the class to ask them, "What have you applied on the job since our training? What have you taken from the course that has led to a modified behavior?" Asking one to two questions of the group will allow for open-ended responses with tangible examples and testimonials of learning transfer. These thoughts post-course can be nuggets of gold.

When learners are given time to reflect and apply their learning, they may come back to you with true work gains that showcase your value as a facilitator. For example, "The technique you taught us in class on how to add interactive experiences to our e-learning courses had measurable gains for our learners in our compliance courses. Thank you for your dedication to ensuring that skill was achieved in the classroom so that we are confidently using it now that we are back on the job."

In facilitating a three-week new-hire training, Darryl lacked the proper feedback to show the impact of the training. Once the learners went out to their regional sites, he would visit after they'd been back on the job 45–60 days. He'd ask them a couple of questions to see how the training went and how it best prepared them for the job. Then, he'd report on those visits monthly to prove the success of the training and directly link it to business impact. The evaluation scores tell only a part of the story, and he wanted to tell the whole story.

What's Next?

The way we give and receive feedback is critical to our continued growth and our impact in our roles. When in doubt, be clear and direct, and offer productive feedback. Don't skip it. Normalize it. Use it frequently as a mechanism for growth and development. And use it so frequently that learners don't even realize the amount of times feedback has been given.

Invitation

Respond to the questions to check in with your current stance on feedback.

1. How do you currently give feedback (to learners, to your team, to yourself)? Think of someone you need to give feedback to. What are two ways in which you could give feedback differently?

   _____

   _____

2. How do you react when you receive feedback? How can you respond differently next time? (Once you answer this question, review your answers for honesty. We give you permission to be real in this answer.)

   _____

   _____

3. What do your evaluation scores (participant surveys) mean to you? How could you interpret them differently moving forward based on this chapter or what has been validated for you?

_____

_____

4. What is one practical technique you want to try when it comes to providing learners feedback in the classroom?

_____

_____

Favorite Social Feeds on Feedback

Because sometimes you need some encouragement, guidance, or quick tips at the drop of a hat when it comes to feedback, we've got you covered! Social feeds and podcasts can deliver great reminders, tips, and general discussions around the art of feedback. We've included some of our favorites below:

A Few Instagram Feeds

- @getleadology for instantaneous feedback tips
- @cliftonstrengths for understanding the unique value each person brings to a situation
- @Iamwellandgood for you, quite simply, because in all the feedback, you need a little you time to maintain positivity

A Few Podcasts

- _Radical Candor_
- _Unlocking Us_ with Brené Brown
- _A Bit of Optimism_ with Simon Sinek
- _On Purpose_ with Jay Shetty
- _Own the Microphone_ with Bridgett McGowen
- _TLDCast: Wired for Connection_
- _The Bob Pike Group_

- *Tiny Leaps, Big Changes*
- ATD's *The Accidental Trainer*
- *The Overnight Trainer*
- *First Time Facilitator*
- *The Happiness Lab*
- ATD's DEI Discussion Series

A Few LinkedIn Communities
- Online Learning Community
- Trainers Network Consulting & Training
- Learning & Development Professionals Club

Chapter 9
Performance Improvement

Performance is why facilitators are called on to help our teams and organizations, and performance is how we prove that our efforts have made an impact. Performance stimulates a training request, is a driver of outcomes and objectives in course design, and is a key marker of training effectiveness both inside and outside the learning space. ATD's *2021 State of the Industry* research report, which highlights talent development benchmarks and trends, revealed that the average organization had a direct learning expenditure of $1,267 per employee in 2020 (ATD 2021a). It's incumbent on facilitators to ensure that spending leads to improved performance through their training delivery.

Let's think of performance in three parts:
- Before the learning experience
- During the learning experience
- After the learning experience

This comprehensive approach to performance is rooted not only in how the learner prepares for, experiences, and applies learning, but in how the manager and facilitator support that effort before, during, and after the learning experience.

Have you ever wondered about how individuals perform after they have completed the training you facilitated? What evidence do you have that your training was successful and people are applying the skills and knowledge they obtained in class back on the job? In this chapter, we'll talk about the facilitator's role in supporting performance before, during, and after the learning experience.

What Is the Facilitator's Role When It Comes to Performance?

Organizations continuously face challenges, from adapting to shifts within the industry to implementing the latest technologies to support digital learning and responding to environmental factors within the organization itself. As trainers and facilitators, we are viewed by many as a key member of the solutions process, whether it is helping the IT department introduce new software equipment to staff or working with the operations department to address current service levels. The facilitator is essential to achieving performance-based outcomes and initiatives. When it comes to impacting performance, the facilitator's role is multifaceted.

We Fulfill Performance Needs

Learners need the ability to develop new knowledge, skills, behaviors, and beliefs over time to unleash true potential. Being a consultative partner during the needs assessment phase of any training initiative is key to fulfilling the performance needs of an individual, a team, and an organization. Carrie can't talk about performance without thinking about the needs assessment to determine what matters to the business, the role, and the individual. She's a firm believer that performance assessed during a training program is only part of a larger system that supports performance improvement back on the job. She has a firm rule to never take on a project unless there is time to do a thorough needs assessment that clearly defines measurable performance criteria and a plan for evaluating success. An added focus for her needs assessment conversations is to uncover how and when the leadership team will promote change in support of the learning experience. Without this information, her role in performance (and not to mention the learners' performance) is most often left unsupported. While you may not have the responsibility of conducting the needs assessment, you want to partner with others to review the results of the needs assessment before you align yourself to any training project.

We Create a Learning Environment Conducive for Performance

Although most learning happens on the job, a facilitator's greatest impact on performance remains in the classroom, in-person or virtual. The learning environment and any activity that occurs in the classroom is what's most directly in our control, and this is our greatest opportunity to impact performance back on the job. Jared believes that because the classroom is the place where we spend the most time interacting with our learners, we should maximize this opportunity by providing the necessary tools and support to learners to succeed when they return to work. If we create a positive learning environment where learners are free to fail and try new things, we can greatly impact their long-term performance. When you use learning objectives to guide your choices in the classroom, then you have a clear pathway to focus your learners' efforts on what matters to their daily success (and to the organization).

Similarly, when it comes to skills practice, simulations, and scenarios, ensure that you are allowing your learners to practice new skills in an environment that closely replicates their reality back on the job. For instance, Carrie once conducted a customer service training to upskill teams on a new system for a financial institution in which her stakeholders had arranged for an in-person classroom training. Upon arriving the morning of the training, Carrie recognized that a quiet classroom with no distractions was not the reality this customer service team faced when performing their job day-to-day. Their reality was a row of standing desks, a floor supervisor pacing the floor available for elevated service calls, bells ringing when quotas were achieved, and each representative fielding customer inquiries through chat, email, and phone at their workstation. This is where they needed to practice the new process:

in an environment closely replicating their on-the-job reality. Otherwise, she would've prepared them to complete a process in an "ideal" setting, not an "authentic" setting.

We Are a Resource

Facilitators might have the greatest impact during the learning experience, but there are significant opportunities before and after the learning takes place to influence and guide our learners. Facilitators can and should remain an ongoing resource to learners.

Nikki recalls the numerous occasions her learners' questions have found their way into her inbox or occurred informally in hallway conversations after the conclusion of a training. She often equips her learners with job aids and checklists that help to support their success back on the job, like case studies, scenarios, or blogs that focus on practical application. The key, she adds, is ensuring that whatever materials and tools you're giving learners to use back on the job, you have trained them on that material so they know how to use the tool to improve performance. Facilitators can leverage the connections made in the classroom to continue supporting learners outside the classroom in small and meaningful ways.

We Are Diligent Observers, Adjusting When Necessary

Despite all our delivery preparation and thoughtful design work, sometimes we need to put aside our best laid plans and adjust for what will maximize performance. Upon hearing of low performance and terminations after providing training to a cohort of learners over two weeks, Darryl was compelled to ensure that the training impacted new employees in fresh and different ways. His creative approach: He began conducting post-training on-site visits 30–45 days after course completion to work directly with learners on applying their new skills and knowledge on the job. The visits informed him on the difference between the training content, real-world job requirements, and environmental factors that might influence their ability to perform. For example, on one visit he heard a colleague share with a new hire, "Don't do it this way; we do it a different way here at this branch."

Darryl modified activities in the training to align more closely with what he had observed during his field visits. As a result, learners were more confident with what they were being asked to do, and he was more successful in equipping learners with the skills and knowledge to be successful in their daily performance.

Why Should Facilitators Embrace Performance-Focused Learning Objectives?

An equally important component for facilitators to master is understanding the purpose of the training and what outcomes we are guiding our learners toward. We hear often in our train-the-trainer programs, "Learners know why they are here. No one wants to review those." or "A slide with bulleted objectives? I'd rather just get right into the content."

When we think of training, the purpose is typically reflected in the learning objectives. Learning objectives are specific, measurable, outcome-based statements that tell the learner what they will be able to do as a result of the training. Learning objectives inform instructional designers on how to structure the lessons, modules, and the overall course, and serve as a tool to guide and evaluate course content development. Learning objectives also inform facilitators, serving as a compass as you move through the content and the experience.

When it comes to course design, you may fall into one of these categories:

- **Hands on.** You are a team of one and you both design and deliver the course. (In short, you're superhuman.)
- **Hands off.** Your course design is done by members of your instructional design team (or contracting firm) and you are typically handed a completed design to bring to life through your delivery of the program. If your trainings are off-the-shelf programs, you fall into this category as well. (You're still superhuman—your skills are just focused elsewhere.)

Whether you are hands on or hands off, you need to understand the importance of learning objectives. Why? Because understanding why and how they are written helps you be more successful in facilitating toward achieving them.

Facilitation in Action

Learning Objectives Provide Direction Toward the Performance-Based Outcome

Nikki worked on a project where a team was implementing a new software system. The subject matter experts (SMEs) wanted to put all learners in a room and share their expertise of the system by providing a demonstration centered on a lecture. Nikki recognized that this method would merely demonstrate a new system, not ensure that learning took place. As a consultative partner in the learning and development process, Nikki stepped in.

She advised the team of the importance of adding learning objectives so there were clear and measurable outcomes that the training would accomplish and that they could evaluate against after the training was complete. The result: The SMEs decided that not everyone in the initial audience would need to be trained (as was initially assumed), saving the company resources and time. They decided to make the course a rolling offering based on those who would be using the system most immediately. The SMEs tweaked their demonstration to be an interactive experience of "show" and "do" where the learners worked through a fictitious case study in a simulated software system to practice all steps of the process in a realistic way. This resulted in the learners getting training when they needed it, and in the context of practical application so that they could hit the ground running as soon as they were assigned their next project.

How Do I Write Effective Learning Objectives?

When we lead ATD's train-the-trainer programs, the conversation around learning objectives is always a standout topic. Regardless of whether our participants identify with the hands-on or hands-off categories, we equip facilitators with the ability to not only review and spot an opportunity for specificity in an objective but to understand how the measurable objective sets the training up for success. Even if the task of creating learning objectives isn't up to the facilitators, it is our responsibility to know what we are training toward.

For Carrie, learning objectives are her compass, her road map, and what allows her to be a consultative partner. When conducting a leadership training for an educational nonprofit, she received the program materials with eight learning objectives all beginning with the verbs "know," "learn," and "understand," followed by one lonely "apply." Immediately she realized that the ability to evaluate success would be limited due to the vagueness of the learning objectives. She scheduled a meeting with the design team to dig into their expectations: "How do we plan on measuring that they know information about intuitive coaching?" That question led the design team to describe what learners would do in the training to demonstrate new knowledge and skill. The probing questions to the design team allowed Carrie to collaborate with them and revise the objectives to provide specific and measurable direction. Let's look at an original objective and a modified objective that aims to be more specific and measurable.

Original objective: Employees will know the stages of appreciative inquiry.

Facilitator thought process: How will I know that they know? How will I measure that they know it? That seems subjective. How will we teach them appreciative inquiry to make sure they know the stages? What do I need to create to make this happen (a wall chart, a game activity, or a visual)? What barriers will prevent them from applying this on the job and how can I tailor my approach to account for that?

Revised objective: Employees will recall five stages of appreciative inquiry using the 5 Ds model and associated activity by the end of the lesson.

Facilitator thought process: OK! So, they need to know the five stages of appreciative inquiry. We'll teach that using the 5 Ds model and the small-group activity, where each group is assigned one of the 5 Ds to explore and teach back to the larger group. We'll assess by doing a matching activity at their table groups using flash cards. By the end of the lesson, they will be able to recall the five stages as we head into our next lesson, which builds off the recall and enables them to put their knowledge into practice. During the debrief I'll conduct a large-group discussion about the potential barriers of implementing on the job. Great!

As we see, this revision allowed the broader learning and development team to align on not only the desired action of the learners (recall) but on what they would do, how they would do it, and what the design team would need to develop. Carrie was also clearer on the goal, and what would need to be leveraged to aid the learners in achieving that objective. Carrie instills in her learners and her colleagues the importance of demystifying learning objectives, adding specificity and ensuring everyone is on the same page regarding what "good" looks like. She explains, "Learning objectives are a great entry point to build consultative partnerships. If I can come to the design team and ask for clarity on a vague objective, I can bring the facilitator's and learner's unique point of view to the discussion." When objectives are clear and specific in a training program, you can go beyond the objective and begin thinking of how to assess what learning took place and help participants transfer the learning to workplace performance.

How Do I Assess Learning?

Performance is constantly assessed, whether that assessment is facilitator to learner, peer to peer, on the job, or learner to facilitator. As you facilitate training, you are looking for signs that your learners are acquiring the knowledge and skills that you demonstrate or that they comprehend the topics being discussed. During training, we use formal tools like skills demonstrations, tests, quizzes, polls, and surveys to test the aptitude of our learners. In addition, we use informal measures like questioning and observation to assess learners' performance or progress. Whether you are responsible for developing training or you're working from content developed by someone else, you want to be aware of how learners will be assessed not only in the training program but when they are back on the job.

As you reflect on classes that you either facilitated or participated in as a learner, you may have seen some formal assessments that didn't quite meet the mark. Maybe the formal assessment had questions unrelated to the topics covered in class. Perhaps a question was worded incorrectly or was confusing. Usually when this happens, the learners aren't shy about letting us know. When we receive this type of feedback from learners, it is often a signal that we lost the intent of the assessment.

For example, while inserting pop culture references into a question for a software training assessment may appear clever and engaging, does this question help to properly assess if our learners obtained the skills and knowledge needed to perform back on the job? For many of you, the answer is a clear and simple no. This doesn't mean we can't be creative. Many assessments suffer from being, dare we say, a bit dry. It's not that they must be hilarious or incredibly engaging, but how can we strive to make them less painful while still ensuring they measure what they intend to measure?

Consider the following perspectives as you build assessments for your programs:

- **Assessment is not an element that occurs just at the end of a lesson or even at the end of the training.** We are constantly assessing throughout. As Nikki reflects on her classes, assessments are not just tests or quizzes used to wrap up the end of a training. She feels that facilitators need to be empowered to think simpler. One of the ways she does this in her programs is through enabling participants to assess fellow learners' performance through feedback during exercise activities. It may be midway through a module in a virtual training and sound like this: "What knowledge check question can you add into the chat box to challenge your fellow learners?" or "What feedback can you provide to one another on the designs you created?" Stepping back and observing what the learners produce for one another is a way to ensure they are all tracking along.

- **Assessments matter less in revealing a score and more in measuring progress and learning.** Carrie takes full advantage of classroom exercises and activities to actively assess learners' practical application of the skills and knowledge they obtain during the program. Adding a debrief discussion centered on the question, "How will this impact your day-to-day performance?" or "How can you apply this in your daily work?" can flip the switch in learners' minds to link the learning experience to their everyday reality in meaningful and practical ways. With these tips in mind, we've curated our go-to assessment techniques as facilitators, adapting them for the virtual and face-to-face classroom (Table 9-1).

Table 9-1. Our Go-To Assessments

Assessment Technique	Outcome	Virtual	Face-to-Face
Test/Quiz	• Check for Understanding • Debrief Exercise	• Virtual Poll • Whiteboard Poll	• Wall Chart • Handout • Interactive Poll
Skills Demonstration (Performance-Based Assessments)	• Link Practice to Performance • Align to Rubric or Checklist	Virtual Skills Demonstration	Skills Demonstration
Debrief Questions	Check for Understanding	• Respond via Chat • Raise Hand • Round Robin	• Share at Table Groups • Share With a Self-Selected Partner • Round Robin

Table 9-1. Our Go-To Assessments (cont)

Assessment Technique	Outcome	Virtual	Face-to-Face
Game-based Activity	• Check for Understanding • Collaborative Learning	Kahoot, Slido, Mentimeter, Poll Everywhere, or Quizlet	• Small Table Group Activity • Kahoot, Slido, Mentimeter, Poll Everywhere, or Quizlet
Explain/Illustrate Connections	Help Learners Link Activities and Discussions to Outcomes of the Course	• Whiteboard Matching Activity • Annotation Activity	• Wall Chart • What's in It for Me (WIIFM) Connection

Assessments should align to learning objectives that align to job performance and closely replicate on-the-job realities.

For Your Consideration

Leveraging Peer-to-Peer Assessments

Imagine you are managing a training program that supports a large maintenance department for a municipality. The maintenance teams are responsible for the grounds of more than 50 facilities within the municipality. You meet periodically with the maintenance leadership team to discuss training needs. One of the crew chiefs shares with you that one of the biggest challenges they encounter is team members incorrectly calculating their gas-to-oil ratios for their lawn mower equipment.

The result of this mistake is a significant percentage of damaged lawn mowers with a large expense to repair or replace. The crew chief feels that verbal reminders to team members are not getting the message across to the team, mainly because there are many team members who are using this type of equipment for the first time. The leadership is proposing a training class to address the issue.

The grounds unit has 100 team members. Twelve of the team members are well versed in using this type of lawn equipment. It is determined that it is too cost prohibitive to bring in an external consultant to train the team. The leadership has scheduled a "training day" and plans on leveraging the experienced personnel to serve as "one-day trainers" to share their knowledge and skills with their peers.

Small groups are formed among team members to receive hands-on demonstrations of how to mix gas and oil to properly operate the lawn mowers. Those with knowledge demonstrated it, and others applied their new knowledge and skills directly in the moment of learning.

Leveraging peer-to-peer assessments and on-the-job learning solved the problem efficiently, and the learners held one another accountable when they returned to the job.

What Barriers Should I Consider When Measuring Performance as a Facilitator?

Let's say that you want to take a proactive approach to measuring performance after your learning event. What does that look like? Whether you are an internal or external trainer, there are barriers that you need to overcome to measure shifts in performance after training. To proactively measure performance requires us to establish relationships with the business lines within our organizations to obtain access and information needed to properly measure performance change.

How cooperative are the business lines at your organization? Do they freely share performance information with you? Do you have the access to move freely around the organization to observe performance? The answer varies for each of us.

Consider the situations we've encountered:

- "A barrier I've encountered is getting the business to cooperate. If I'm working on a project as a part of the internal staff, I have access to business partners who are telling me not to have more consultative conversations. If I'm contracted to facilitate for an organization and am bringing an outside perspective, I have to work with multiple individuals to get answers, which inevitably moves my timeline."—Jared

- "You have to be knowledgeable of the business. I forge relationships across the organization at all levels with the intent to go out from my office and observe performance in person in the individual's environment. This allows me to bring realistic and practical approaches to my facilitation."—Darryl
- "As an external facilitator, you bring a different perspective to the project. You have a bit of bargaining influence where you can set clear boundaries and expectations on how you will measure performance after training. You also have the luxury of setting the parameters of your partnership and only committing to support learning programs that consider strategies for implementing and supporting change management post-training."—Carrie

As facilitators, we continually strive to develop business acumen—an in-depth understanding of how the business works—because this knowledge helps us make more informed decisions during training delivery. Carrie uses the analogy of a keyhole. "As a facilitator, I'm often invited to look through the keyhole into the business drivers that inform the training. I have limited peripheral, and my ability to see detail and context is limited to what I've been given access to. My goal is to see the collective business, to get inside the room and move around, open windows, adjust the lighting, and rearrange the furniture to understand the full scope of the business request."

What Is Our Role in Coaching and Mentoring and How Do They Impact Performance?

This is a question we hear from ATD learners all the time. According to the TD Body of Knowledge, coaching and mentoring are distinguished as follows:

- **Coaching** is a widely used term with multiple definitions. The International Coaching Federation (2022) defines coaching as "a professional partnership between a qualified coach and an individual or team that supports the achievement of extraordinary results, based on goals set by the individual or team. Through the process of coaching, individuals focus on the skills and actions needed to successfully produce their personally relevant results." It is not counseling, mentoring, training, or giving advice. Coaching may also be used on the job, when a more experienced person, often a supervisor, provides constructive advice and feedback to develop or improve an employee's performance.

- **Mentoring** is a development opportunity that encompasses receiving valuable information, guidance, and feedback from an experienced individual to gain understanding of organizational culture and unwritten norms.

Coaching and mentoring are both by-products of the work we do in learning and development to forge relationships and make ourselves available after training to be an ongoing resource. The more successful we are at creating a positive learning environment, the more likely we are to receive post-training requests for ongoing conversations, guidance, and private Q&A sessions to continue the partnership in learning. So, coaching and mentoring are key components to the facilitator's approach to improving performance.

To get a sense of the frequency with which coaching is used in an organization, research reveals that 61 percent of organizations are using coaching as a performance support tool before or after training programs. And trainers spend 46 percent of their classroom time facilitating engaging learning activities, coaching, or giving feedback to learners (ATD 2020).

For Your Consideration

The Facilitator's Perspective on the Nuances Between Coaching and Mentoring

Coaching is a discipline that focuses on goals and objectives, is interactive in its approach to building skills and awareness, and uses specific tools to achieve results. It can be part of a larger strategy to help individuals, units, systems, and organizations make improvements to performance. The facilitator's role could be leading structured peer-to-peer coaching sessions for continued performance support, modeling new skills in the workflow, coaching individuals through performance obstacles, or setting up post-training support to guide learners in creating action plans and applying new skills or knowledge.

Mentoring is a partnership that focuses on relationship building, sharing, and learning from one another, in an effort to develop the self through the influence of others. When you mentor an individual, consider showing up for a conversation that is less structured and more informal, and share practical experiences, leveraging stories and examples, as the person needs them to guide their discovery.

Both methods allow us to be in partnership with the learner and the organization to increase performance outside of the training space and aid in change management and learning transfer.

How Do I Build Coaching and Mentoring Opportunities Into My Programs?

We feel this is such a great question, and always appreciate the opportunity to respond to it during our trainings, because it's focused on supporting performance and continued learning. First, gain clarity around the expectations and parameters of the relationship, including organizational and leadership support. What are the expectations of all parties? What's the purpose or intended outcome of the support? What are the metrics for success?

Consider the following examples for ways to incorporate formal and informal opportunities for coaching and mentoring for your learners.

Formal Coaching

Carrie was working with an organization that developed a coaching program to support new hires in a field sales capacity. The program was designed to ensure new hires were exposed to the realities of the job in the field alongside a high-performing coach who could demonstrate behaviors and model expectations. The program was designed with clear goals for the coaching relationship, detailed guidelines and expectations for both the coach and coachee, and an evaluative process that triggered additional coaching sessions or a release into the field to fulfill the role in full capacity. The program not only created partnerships across field sales teams, increasing employee engagement, but the coaching partnerships were naturally extending beyond the initial agreement in informal follow-up conversations. The program allowed learners to observe behaviors, perform them, and get instantaneous feedback on areas of improvement and focus from a trusted resource who performed the same job. In short, the coaching program allowed the coach to help translate the policies, procedures, and best practices of the onboarding training into the reality of the workplace. The program was not only successful in yielding an increased sales performance from new hires in the first 90 days in the role, but it became a coaching model that began to be leveraged throughout the organization for other roles as well.

Formal Mentoring

In a previous role in retail banking, Darryl was a mentee in the High Potential Employee (HPE) Mentoring Program. The program was administered by the company's HR and training departments and was designed to help HPEs's readiness to apply for leadership opportunities within the company. It provided a unique opportunity where HPEs were paired with senior leaders to build their development path.

The training department first met with senior leaders to "mentor the mentor." This was an opportunity to outline the mentor's responsibilities and to walk them through the mentoring process. The mentor was introduced to several approaches (learning paths) that they could potentially offer to support their mentee. Some examples of approaches that were introduced included leadership development and personal branding.

The HR department was responsible for selection of HPE mentees and matching them with their mentor. Once the pairs were identified, the company sponsored a luncheon that served as the official kickoff for the program. HR and training outlined a specific mentoring process for participants to follow but left the parameters on how often the mentor and mentee were to meet to each partnership. HR and training teamed to send the mentees periodic progress surveys (after months two and six) to measure progress of the mentee's goals and objectives for the program. A structured mentorship program requires the time and attention of senior leaders to invest in the future leaders of the company.

Informal Coaching

While working at an advertising agency, Jared conducted a manager experience analysis as a part of a project to establish a peer-to-peer network in support of skill building across the organization. The goal was to develop an understanding of what it was like to be a people manager at the agency. One of the key findings was that managers felt alone; they didn't have anyone to speak to about the day-to-day happenings on their teams. Partnering with the HR team, Jared saw the opportunity to create a manager network.

The goal was to provide opportunities for people managers to connect and build relationships with one another, forming a sense of community that employees stated was missing. It started off formalized, with structured physical and digital experiences so the managers could meet and begin building relationships. Unique programming with guest speakers and learning opportunities was organized for several months to kick off the initiative. Over time, the network needed less-formal experiences as connections within the group began to spring to life. Organic posts in the Teams channel asking for advice or sharing resources became more common and integrated into daily work. Volunteering to make introductions or set up happy hours or experiences became normalized. Managers who had felt alone were now actively supporting and developing one another. The success of the network came from a balance of formal and informal approaches. The magic, though, was when the organizers saw the opportunity to move to the background and provide the managers the opportunity to engage in the network and make it work for them.

Informal Mentoring

During training experiences, Nikki empowers learners to apply their knowledge throughout their time together as well as make an action plan for how they will implement their learning when they leave the classroom. She sets expectations around the fact that she is there to guide and support them through their learning journeys before, during, and after the program. She encourages them to not only network and maintain relationships with her but do the same with one another: "You have many like-minded colleagues in the room; make connections and mentor each other after our time ends."

For training on e-learning authoring tools, she encourages learners to share their created e-learning modules post-program, and she commits to offering them support as they navigate implementing the skills when they are back on the job. Nikki has had learners reach out to troubleshoot errors; request reminder prompts of steps of a process; seek recommendations on resources, tools, or templates; and even review created e-learning modules. She works in an informal mentoring pattern to support their needs and sets clear boundaries for herself and the learner when the relationship may need to lessen or dissolve.

What's Next?

Performance is an accomplishment of an activity, and simultaneously it's a journey of small successes, mishaps and stumbles, and continued development. Performance should not be based on a single assessment. Can you imagine what it would be like if it were? Being defined by a single instance or score where you didn't perform your best? Performance encompasses not only a moment in time performing on the job, but a broader scope of various efforts over time, trends in performance, improvements, effort output (or lack of effort), and any tangible data that helps tell the story of an individual's (and the organization's) performance.

Invitation

1. What's the most common type of assessment used in your training programs? What new assessment approach would you like to incorporate into
   your training?

   _____

   _____

2. Consider how you can turn an assessment opportunity into an ongoing
   journey for the learner. Can you frame an assessment of skills and knowledge as the beginning of a continual effort to show improvement? Would
   that change the results?

   _____

   _____

3. What performance support measures will you use to supplement performance? Whom will you partner with?

   _____

   _____

4. How will you measure progress or learning throughout the training?

   _____

   _____

Chapter 10
Future Readiness and Lifelong Learning

In this chapter, and as we near the end of this book, let's shift our focus to the journey we take as facilitators to continually upskill, reskill, and demonstrate agility in meeting the needs of the learner, the organization, and the self. This is, in fact, the one time in our profession when it's OK not to focus on the outcomes and instead turn our attention to the journey.

Facilitators, by the very nature of what we do, are some of the most selfless and passionate individuals. Facilitators give up sleep and convenience, bypass lunch and adequate breaks to make time to help learners, and even give to learners what last bit of energy they have. Facilitators will bend over backward to show up for learners in the most authentic ways. But let me ask you: When was the last time you gave yourself that same attention and energy?

We must continually remind ourselves that we are practitioners at our core. As a necessity, we should be ongoing learners. But how do we make time and prioritize our own learning over our passion to help others learn? More important, how do we find the discipline and energy to allow ourselves to become learners? How do we show up, sit down, and give in to the fine art of learning?

As facilitators, we aim for more moments of self-actualization in our classroom, hoping to help our participants arrive at their own discoveries, and even planning the mini parade for when they do. More learner motivation! More ahas! More behavior change! And in that fearless pursuit, we forget that we too are learners; and even if we don't forget, we merely shuffle it down the priority list because we show up for our learners more than we do for ourselves.

That stops today!

Future Readiness

Future readiness requires intellectual curiosity and constant scanning of the environment to stay abreast of forces shaping the business world, employees and their expectations, and the talent development profession (ATD 2019). As Peter Senge, a thought leader in the field of organizational learning and systems thinking, states (2010), "People with a high level of personal mastery live in a continual learning mode. They never 'arrive.'" Here's to never arriving!

Future readiness can sound, perhaps ironically, a little unpredictable. It isn't about gazing into the crystal ball and uttering the words, "I see . . . " while making wild predictions of what could happen. As far as we know today, no one can tell us what will happen in the future. This means that future readiness depends on analyzing current problems and trends and identifying potential or likely responses in a given industry, organization, or role.

As facilitators, we aim to remain curious about new and better ways to deliver learning experiences, we stay on top of industry trends through our own study and networking, and we remain vigilant in our pursuit of constant upskilling and reskilling to evolve alongside the industry and those we lead in our training programs. Our facilitation team at ATD makes it a practice to bring learner insights gleaned from course deliveries to our team meetings, in addition to sharing new tools and approaches with one another. We value and make space for the conversations around what we glean from our learners, which allows us to operate from a position of readiness, present or future.

There are events that rapidly impact the lives of every individual in our organizations. Facilitators play a necessary role in how organizations react and respond to the unexpected, whether it is the 2007 financial crisis, the 2020 COVID-19 pandemic, or a new chief executive officer for your company. Future readiness for facilitators is proactively preparing to encounter rapid or sudden change within our organizations. We model this through our ability to always be ready for whatever comes next. In turn, we show the workforce how to respond positively to new demands of the organization.

Lifelong Learning

Lifelong learning is the ongoing, self-motivated quest for knowledge to develop both personally and professionally. Lifelong learning can include traits such as self-motivation, insatiable curiosity, and intelligent risk-taking. In a 2018 report on the topic, ATD Research identified a number of behaviors demonstrated by lifelong learners. We've included ideas for enhancing your facilitator skills based on that research.

- **Ask questions.** Practice innate curiosity with learners as well as stakeholders. Lead with *why* questions to understand the thinking and the influencing factors that contributed to an action or a behavior. Lead with *how* questions to dig into opportunities to challenge how we think outcomes can be achieved. Carrie adds in a component of asking *what if* questions to test possibilities and barriers in partnership conversations.

- **Experiment and try new things.** Start a challenge on your facilitator team to use a new app or collaboration tool each session. Challenge your beliefs of how a program can be facilitated. We do this often on our team and are continuously learning from one another by trying new things.

- **Seek resources and do your own research.** This ties directly to practicing innate curiosity. Within that curiosity is an opportunity to seek out new perspectives, new resources, and research that supports an approach. Mostly, know what the field is in conversation about. Better yet, engage in that conversation.

- **Apply new knowledge.** For every skill, technique, tool, or methodology you learn, ensure it has a linked behavior or action. You can read all the articles on adaptive learning that are circulating, but if you don't translate it into action or changed behavior, you're merely hoarding information in your brain (and that thing needs a break!).
- **Share knowledge and teach others.** Don't be a hoarder! You know those dogs that run around and stockpile all the toys near them, merely to prevent other dogs from playing with them? Don't stockpile the toys! Share your knowledge, your tools, your resources, and your key learnings with others and broaden your network of practical experience when they return the favor. You'll find that as you share and invite more people into that conversation, they will build on the idea or knowledge and, in turn, you'll learn from their contributions. Everything we learn and practice as facilitators originates from every trainer we've observed, been mentored by, and worked alongside.

What Have Been the Biggest Changes to the Trainer's Role in the Past Five Years?

The pace of change, as we spoke about at the beginning of this book, is ever evolving across the talent development landscape. Future readiness and lifelong learning are essential skills and mindsets that facilitators must not only embrace for their own personal and professional development, but model for their learners. There are two core questions around this topic that we hear most from our learners in ATD Education programs. Let's start with what the biggest changes have been in the last five years:

- **From expert to network.** There's been a continuous shift from expert to network. Facilitators are still expected to be experts or have credibility in their topic, but our learners' expectations have grown beyond just this—they demand more. Jared explains that it is less about "Can you answer all my questions?" and more about "Who or what can you connect me with to help me grow?" The role of facilitators is shifting into that of providing access, whether that is to content, people, or opportunities. The nature of our roles usually gives us a wider view than the average employee. We may work across departments, offices, and teams, and that exposure now comes with a responsibility to share what we are learning with our learners. We are less a provider of information and more a catalyst for connections.

- **Facilitators = leaders.** The facilitator's role has continued to expand beyond the classroom and trickle into daily workplace interactions, solidifying their role as influencers. Facilitators are constantly called on to be leaders. Leaders in asking questions—questions whose answers may lead us somewhere we've never been. Leaders in redefining roles in a world thrust into asynchronous communications and hybrid learning. Leaders in examining the efficacy of what's considered traditional. There have been new challenges presented, and these challenges had no checklists or success stories to influence their outcome. We're in a time of new thinking, a time for the collective to lead, and facilitators by the nature of our role are most equipped to do that. This requires us to peek outside the classroom, so to speak, and begin engaging in consultative partnerships with finance, IT, leadership, and customer service.

- **Flexibility for improving learning transfer.** The facilitator's role requires less rigidity; instead, it demands a constant model of flexibility to leverage technology changes and collaborative team efforts to improve learning transfer. A facilitator may now start the day reviewing materials, trying out a new tech tool, communicating with key stakeholders as a collaborative partner, and providing feedback to learners in an empathic way. They come to their learners as teammates to work together to accomplish shared goals in a respectful and engaging manner. With this shift, Nikki has noticed that trainers are more enthusiastic about their roles and the empowerment to make a difference rather than getting stale and burned out on repeating the same topics, content, and courses over and over without the opportunity to grow.

- **Continued emergence of technology.** The emergence of technology has provided learners with more choices to learn in the workplace in both formal and informal learning experiences. For Darryl, this means learners have more access to communicate with facilitators and fellow learners before, during, and after the training, which opens up the opportunity for more one-on-one coaching and on-the-job instruction.

What Do We Need to Look Ahead To?

As we reflect on the changes that have occurred, we can also begin looking ahead:

- **Enhanced agility.** Facilitators need advanced methods of agility, not only in our approach and our thinking, but how we execute our role. Pivoting in facilitation is not a "nice to have" or "mastery" level skill, according to Carrie. Pivoting is an essential skill for effective facilitation to align to the needs of the workforce and the organization. Additionally, Carrie anticipates a look to wellness (mindset, creativity, well-being) across learning experiences, as we continue to strive for inclusivity, accessibility, and equity in our learning programs. She also anticipates a continued shift toward the individual being accountable for their development, so fostering a culture that encourages advocating for growth and professional development will become an essential skill.
- **Cultivate your community.** Skills in cultivating a network of peers inside and outside of your organization will continue to be essential to our roles. Darryl believes being around others who share a passion for our craft provides a source of fresh ideas and perspectives to help in our role, as well as a

gut check against things we're reluctant to embrace or try. The facilitator's role constantly evolves, which demands us as individuals to evolve. Our network can provide new insights we may not have considered.

- **From specialist to generalist.** Talent development will become less dominated by formal learning facilitation time and see an uptick in more blended experiences mixing asynchronous and synchronous environments to closely replicate learners' real-life work scenarios. With this shift, Jared envisions there will be a migration from specialist to generalist for many in talent development, including facilitators. We'll need to be fluent in the holistic learning process (as opposed to merely aware of it) to impact more than the learning experience and continue influencing performance across the organization.

- **Your why will become central.** Understanding your why will be essential to navigating the evolution of talent development. The learners still need to remain front and center to the facilitator—they are our why. That is what guides all the decisions we make in the classroom. We must be comfortable trying out one technique at a time, and adjusting, changing, and modifying accordingly. Remember your why always. Develop a mantra as a facilitator and state it each time you prepare for your programs, because this will help to keep you authentic and relatable.

What's Next?

The pace of change in the talent development industry—now more so than ever since March 2020, when most of the workforce rapidly shifted to remote work, hybrid work, and highly virtual experiences—requires constant upskilling and reskilling of the workforce. We've shared some tips to get your thinking started. What would you add?

- **Own your professional development.** Create a vision, set a learning path, and reach out to those who can partner with you in your ongoing development. Not sure where to start? You have four new colleagues (us!) to be a part of your network.

- **Find your fear and master it.** Are you fearful of e-learning or technology apps in the classroom? Dig your heels in, read articles, talk to other trainers, and make it your specialty.
- **Identify your top five skills as a facilitator.** Then, identify your top five areas of opportunity. The key here? Center your efforts on developing both continuously.
- **Establish credibility.** Do this in a way that's authentic to you. If you would like to be a credential holder like Nikki, obtain a professional certification in your field. If you would like to mentor a new trainer within or outside of your organization like Darryl, take steps to give back in a way that works for you. If you love homing in on specialized topics in our field, such as strengths-based leadership (like Carrie), earn a specialization in a topic of interest that can inform your impact. If you know you can bring your best self to work through an identified purpose like Jared, take time to establish credibility in leading projects with that in mind.
- **Establish your voice in the talent development landscape.** Whether you enjoy writing blogs, moderating interviews and panels, or conducting webinars, find an avenue to contribute to the conversation or come together with other professionals. Intentionally participating in industry events, seminars, local organization communities, or workshops (more than a business card swap or LinkedIn connection) can present an opportunity to connect with others and determine how you can work together.
- **Find a platform that feels authentic and natural to you.** And then build your network, focusing on engagement. We know, this can at times feel challenging to some. But this is in part your social, personal brand we're talking about. Respond to articles and conversations, engage with peers (new and old) on those discussion threads—this is an excellent way to begin the

conversation. We would be remiss if we didn't point out that social platforms are littered with "thought leaders." Ensure their contributions are rooted in practical experience before you buy in on ideas shared.

Above all else, embrace the notion at the start of this chapter from Peter Senge of "never arriving." And know that on this continuous path of personal and professional development, we welcome you to walk alongside us, to continue exploring, to continue championing talent development. This is, in fact, the greatest and most thrilling journey of them all. As facilitators, we have the unique responsibility and privilege of influencing the way individuals show up in their daily lives.

References

Addington, C. 2019. "Keep It Real." *TD*, September. td.org/magazines/td
-magazine/keep-it-real.

"ATD Master Trainer Program." Education program from the Association
for Talent Development. td.org/education-courses/atd-master
-trainer-program.

ATD (Association for Talent Development). 2018. *Lifelong Learning: The
Path to Personal and Organizational Performance*. Alexandria, VA:
ATD Press.

ATD (Association for Talent Development). 2019. *Effective Evaluation:
Measuring Learning Programs for Success*. Alexandria, VA:
ATD Press.

ATD (Association for Talent Development). 2020. *Effective Trainers:
Traditional and Virtual Classroom Success*. Alexandria, VA: ATD Press.

ATD (Association for Talent Development). 2021a. *2021 State of the
Industry*. Alexandria, VA: ATD Press.

ATD (Association for Talent Development). 2021b. *Virtual Classrooms:
Leveraging Technology for Impact*. Alexandria, VA: ATD Press.

ATD (Association for Talent Development). 2019. Talent Development
Body of Knowledge. Alexandria, VA: ATD.

"Talent Development Glossary Terms." ATD. td.org/glossary-terms.

Biech, E. 2005. *Training for Dummies*. Hoboken, NJ: Wiley Publishing.

Buckingham, M., and A. Goodall. 2019. "The Feedback Fallacy." *Harvard
Business Review*, March-April. hbr.org/2019/03/the-feedback-fallacy.

David, S. 2017. "The Gift and Power of Emotional Courage." TEDWoman 2017, November. Video. ted.com/talks/susan_david_the_gift_and _power_of_emotional_courage/transcript?language=en.

Defelice, R. 2021. "How Long Does It Take to Develop Training? New Question, New Answers." ATD blog, January 13. td.org/insights /how-long-does-it-take-to-develop-training-new-question-new -answers.

Dhawan, E. 2021. *Digital Body Language: How to Build Trust and Connection, No Matter the Distance.* New York: St. Martin's Press.

Dweck, C. 2007. *Mindset: The New Psychology of Success.* New York: Ballantine Books.

Gottfredson, R. 2022. "The Irreplaceable Growth Mindset." Chapter 8 in *ATD's Handbook for Training and Talent Development,* edited by E. Biech. Alexandria, VA: ATD Press.

Huggett, C. 2021. "2022 State of Virtual Training." Infographic. Cindy Huggett, December. cindyhuggett.com/wp-content/uploads /2021/12/2022-State-of-Virtual-Training-Infographic-from -Cindy-Huggett.pdf.

ICF (International Coaching Federation). 2022. "What Is Coaching?" About ICF. coachingfederation.org/about.

Knowles, M.S. 1984. *Andragogy in Action.* San Francisco: Jossey-Bass.

LaBorie, K., and T. Stone. 2022. *Interact and Engage! 75+ Activities for Virtual Training, Meetings, and Webinars.* Alexandria, VA: ATD Press.

Langford, J., and P.R. Clance. 1993. "The Impostor Phenomenon: Recent Research Findings Regarding Dynamics, Personality and Family Patterns and Their Implications for Treatment." *Psychotherapy: Theory, Research, Practice, Training* 30(3): 495–501.

Maslow, A.H. 1943. "A Theory of Human Motivation." *Psychological Review* 50(4): 370–396.

Medina, J. 2008. *Brain Rules: 12 Principles for Surviving and Thriving at Work, Home, and School.* Seattle, WA: Pear Press.

"Facilitating." Merriam-Webster Online. merriam-webster.com /dictionary/facilitating.

"Training." Merriam-Webster Online. merriam-webster.com/dictionary /training.

Morukian, M. 2022. *Diversity, Equity, and Inclusion for Trainers.* Alexandria, VA: ATD Press.

Navarro, J. 2019. "Former FBI Agent Explains How to Read Body Language." *Wired*, May 21. Video. youtube.com/watch?v=4jw UXV4QaTw.

NIST (National Institute of Standards and Technology). 2015. "Ritz-Carlton Practices for Building a World-Class Service Culture." The Official Baldrige Blog, March 16. nist.gov/blogs/blogrige /ritz-carlton-practices-building-world-class-service-culture.

O'Keeffe, N. 2019. "My 'Meeting Learners Where They Are' Moment." ATD blog, March 5. td.org/insights/my-meeting-learners-where -they-are-moment.

O'Keeffe, N. 2020a. "Be Intentional and Realistic as a Department of One." *TD*, February. td.org/magazines/td-magazine/be-intentional -and-realistic-as-a-department-of-one.

O'Keeffe, N. 2020b. "Boost Learner Engagement in the Virtual Classroom." *TD*, December. td.org/magazines/td-magazine/boost -learner-engagement-in-the-virtual-classroom.

O'Keeffe, N. 2020c. "Recover From Online Training Disruptions." *TD*, December. td.org/magazines/td-magazine/recover-from-online -training-disruptions.

Rickenback, R. 2016. "Do You Know the Difference Between Training and Facilitation?" ATD blog, July 6. td.org/atd-blog/do-you-know -the-difference-between-training-and-facilitation.

Rogers, C. 1951. *Client-Centered Therapy: Its Current Practice, Implications and Theory*. London: Constable.

Senge, P. 2010. *The Fifth Discipline: The Art & Practice of The Learning Organization*. New York: Currency.

St. Louis, M. 2017. "Research Shows That the Clothes You Wear Actually Change the Way You Perform." *Inc*, June 8. inc.com/molly-reynolds /research-shows-that-the-clothes-you-wear-actually-change-the-way-you-perform.html.

Steffey, D. Vital Signs Training. linkedin.com/in/ donna-steffey-mba-cptd-898921.

Stone, D., and S. Heen. 2014. *Thanks for the Feedback: The Science and Art of Receiving Feedback Well.* New York: Penguin Books.

Wigert, B., and N. Dvorak. 2019. "Feedback Is Not Enough." Gallup Workplace blog, May 16. gallup.com/workplace/257582/feedback -not-enough.aspx.

Index

Page numbers followed by *t* and *f* refer to tables and figures.

encouraging, in face-to-face classrooms, 80
feedback through, 149
disruptions, 90–91
distractions, avoiding, 68
diversity, defined, 117
Diversity, Equity, and Inclusion for Trainers (Morukian), 120
diversity, equity, and inclusion (DEI) initiatives, 117, 137–138
Do (in FOID model), 112
Dweck, Carol, 2

E

Effective Evaluation (ATD), 54
Effective Trainers (ATD), 43
e-learning, 178
electronic polls, 149
emails, introduction, 29
empathetic facilitation
about, 120–122
and adult learning principles,
118–120
example, 122–123
empathy. *See also* empathetic facilitation
activities to build, 131–137
defining, 117–118
empowerment, 55, 56
energizers, 131–132
engagement
questioning techniques to increase,
112
using pre-work for, 30
in virtual classrooms, 77–78, 87–90
environment(s)
facilitator role in creating safe and
positive, 49–52
managing the, 19–20
for virtual classrooms, 77

equity, defined, 117–118
event (term), 44
examples and analogies
inclusive and empathetic, 126
tailoring, in face-to-face classrooms, 79
expectations, setting, 48–49
experience (term), 44
explain/illustrate connections (assessment technique), 171*t*

F

face-to-face classrooms, 79–86
adaptations for, 79–83
assessments in, 170*t*–171*t*
defined, 76
environment for, 19–20
host/sponsor communication for,
22
moving to virtual from, 91–94
overcoming challenges in, 83–85
preparing for, 38–40
sample, 85–86
technology in, 20
facilitation, 1–17
case example, 13–15
feedback as enabler for, 8–9
and fixed vs. growth mindset, 2–3
mindset for, 1–2
moving from good to great, 3–5
and pivoting in the moment, 7–8
and role of facilitators (*See* facilitator role)
styles of (*See* facilitation styles)
training vs., 9–13, 11*t*
facilitation styles, 61–73
and adapting to change, 70–72
building confidence in, 64–68
importance of, 61–62
intuition vs. intention in, 68–70
types of, 62–64

temperature, 21

tests, 170*t*

Thanks for the Feedback (Stone), 140–141

Throw It Out (icebreaker), 134–135

timing, 45–47
  for instruction develop, 47*t*
  pivoting for, 108*t*
  and setting realistic commitments, 46–47
  and timing charts, 40–41

tone, 21

training, facilitation vs., 9–13, 11*t*

U

unscheduled break, 84

V

videos, in asynchronous online environments, 96–97

virtual classrooms, 86–94
  adaptations for, 86–87
  adjusting from face-to-face to, 91–94
  assessments in, 170*t*–171*t*
  body language in, 130
  challenges managed in, 90–91
  confidence in, 67–68
  defined, 76
  engagement in, 87–90
  preparing for, 40–41
  time to develop instruction for, 47*t*

Virtual Classrooms (ATD), 86

virtual producers, communication with, 23–25

Vital Signs Consulting, 112

volunteering, 4–5

vulnerability, 122

W

why, importance of your, 187

workspace. *See* environment(s)

Wow and How About, 147, 150

About the Authors

Carrie Addington is senior manager of learning experience and facilitator development at ATD, where she leads the strategy for the facilitation and learning experience of ATD education courses. She is a master facilitator and strengths-based people development coach with a passion for delivering practical learning experiences with a spirited energy. As an education consultant and facilitator for more than 12 years, Carrie has worked with a variety of business segments including retail, beauty, education, and nonprofits, and has worked with C-level executives, directors, managers, and high potentials.

As a certified ATD Master Trainer and ATD Master Instructional Designer, Carrie is knowledgeable about both the development and delivery of outcome-based learning programs and thrives on creating bespoke learning solutions that yield business impact.

Carrie has delivered on topics ranging from energetic accountability, leadership, and great feedback to resolving conflict and train-the-trainer programs. As a global speaker, Carrie is passionate about training delivery and facilitation, speaking on topics like daring facilitation and overcoming challenging classroom behaviors.

She has a master of fine arts, poetry is passionate about using her love of language and the arts to work with individuals on establishing deeper connections with their daily work.

Jared Douglas is an internal ATD facilitator. He uses a learner-centric approach to create an engaging, inclusive environment in his sessions. As a consultant, Jared has worked with organizations across various industries, including advertising, transportation, finance, technology, and consumer goods, to help clients develop and execute in-person, digital, and blended learning initiatives.

Leading the North American learning function for Momentum Worldwide, a global experiential advertising agency, Jared was responsible for the full-cycle learning experience. This included needs analysis, development and sourcing of content, curriculum building, logistics and coordination of learning programs, and evaluating for effectiveness. He built a variety of courses, facilitated open enrollment and bespoke team workshops, and contributed to various projects such as launching an employee experience brand and redesigning the performance management process.

Jared has facilitated on a range of topics, including communication skills, collaboration, relationship building, brainstorming, client mapping, time management, and presentation skills. He earned a bachelor's degree in psychology from Binghamton University and a master's in industrial and organizational psychology from Baruch College. Jared is fascinated by psychological perspectives and enjoys connecting theoretical content with practical and relevant applications in day-to-day activities.

Nikki O'Keeffe is program manager of facilitator development at ATD. As a certified ATD Master Trainer, ATD Master Instructional Designer, and APTD credential holder, she understands the value of solid training plans and strong facilitation. Having served many years as a facilitator for ATD's face-to-face, online, and asynchronous certificate programs. In addition to her facilitation, she supports ATD's global facilitator network with performance support to ensure each delivery for ATD participants is impactful. Nikki looks forward to sharing her experiences and expanding her knowledge base by learning from the participants, business partners, and co-facilitators in the ATD courses that she designs, develops, and facilitates. Nikki's mission statement is, "To connect, motivate, and challenge talent development professionals to be the best version of themselves."

Darryl Wyles is a facilitator for ATD with more than 20 years of experience in talent development. He has played major roles in transforming learning programs as a leader for large and small organizations in government and the financial services industry. Darryl enjoys the challenge of building organizational end-to-end training solutions from the ground up and is passionate about providing a fun and interactive learning environment in his workshops.

Prior to his current role, Darryl was the training and development manager for the Maryland–National Capital Park and Planning Commission, Department of Parks and Recreation, where he spearheaded the creation of Parks and Recreation University, the department's first structured training and development program. Parks and Recreation University introduced a wide variety of leadership and skill development learning programming that enhanced workforce's proficiencies and expertise.

Darryl has a bachelor's degree in interdisciplinary studies, sports management, from the University of Maryland Baltimore County.